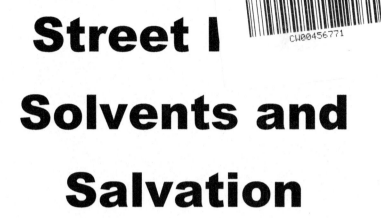

Street I
Solvents and
Salvation

An Inspirational
True Story

by

Natalie Vellacott

List of Ports in order of Logos Hope Schedule

1 Penang, Malaysia
2 Port Klang, Malaysia
3 Kuching, Malaysia
4 Kota Kinabalu, Malaysia
5 Singapore, Singapore
6 Cebu, Philippines

7 Manila, Philippines
8 Subic Bay, Philippines
9 Hong Kong, SAR China
10 Sihanoukville, Cambodia
11 Bangkok, Thailand
12 Hong Kong, SAR China
13 San Fernando, Philippines

14 Subic Bay, Philippines
15 Puerto Princesa
16 Kuching Malaysia
17 Singapore, Singapore
18 Phuket, Thailand
19 Colombo, Sri Lanka

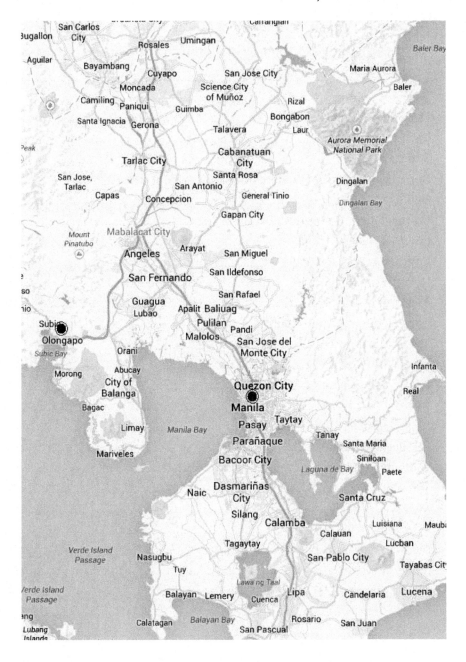

Contents

Introduction 6

The Bridge 8

The "Rugby Boys" 12

The Bridge Team 15

The Leaders 22

The Young Ones 29

Department of Social Welfare and Development (DSWD) 32

Dentist to the Rescue 35

Consolidating the Friendships 39

Practical Help 43

Internet Access and Social Media 46

Living at the Hospital 49

Breaches of Trust 53

Gang Fight and Other Trouble 59

The Real Stories 64

Mark: The Prodigal Son 69

Paul: A Special Friendship 77

Loss of Control 84

Local Churches: Please Help Us! 87

Feeding Programme 90

Teething Problems 94

The Worst Day 100

My Favourite Day 104

New Beginnings 111

Division and Destruction 116

Mixed Emotions 120

My Big Mistake 124

Final Farewells 128

Rehab 133

Bonus Visit 138

Good News and Bad News 142

Logos Hope Returns 145

Miles Apart 151

Olongapo Christian Help and Hope 154

Centre for Youth 157

Reunited 160
Rugby Boys in Church 166
My Wake Up Call 170
Grading Celebration Day 174
End of an Era 178
Epilogue 183
The Individuals 185
Natalie's Story 192
The Wordless Book 194

Introduction

In late September 2011, I excitedly walked with approximately seventy-five others, up the gangway of the Logos Hope Christian missionary ship, for the first time. The ship was in Penang, Malaysia having just begun its tour of South East Asia. Prior to my enquiries in relation to this commitment, I had not heard of the ship and had never been to Asia. I was also ignorant of a large group of islands in the region known as the Philippines. My English friends will not be too surprised, as prior to this point, I wasn't sure where Wales was and had confused Lakeside with the Lake District.

On making my journey into the unknown, I knew only that the ship was said to be the largest floating Book-fair in the world, and that it was to be my home for the next two years. I was to live and work on-board with four hundred fellow born-again Christians, from a total of sixty-five nationalities. The saving grace, for me anyway, was that the commonly spoken language on-board was English. The ship travels from port to port, remaining for about three weeks in each, and then from country to country, to bring knowledge, help and hope to the residents of each place. The floating Book-fair, being the largest in the world, provides knowledge through a wide selection of reasonably priced books. They include; Christian, educational, hobbies, cookery, novels and anything else you can think of. The crew member volunteers help local people through practical work, medical and dental missions, donations of food and other items, and in other ways. Every crew member has a story of how Jesus has changed their life personally. They seek to share their testimonies, with both the visitors to the Book-fair and the people they meet whilst on-shore, bringing hope to all nations of the world. From the outset, it was the "hope" part that I was most interested in.

This story really begins, on March 12th, 2012, when the Logos Hope sailed into a lesser known part of the world called Subic Bay, in the Philippines. It should have been just another port in one of many countries. The only planned difference was that the ship was due for its mandatory annual servicing and maintenance whilst stationed in the port, and some major repairs were required. Still, the scheduled time in the dry dock was just a little over two months, which seemed reasonable. For the work to be carried out, and the ship to be properly inspected, it had to be partially lifted out of the water, hence the term "dry dock."

Many things happened after this date to keep the ship in Subic Bay far beyond its intended stay, and even when it did eventually break free and sail on to new pastures, it wasn't long before it would be back. It seems there was a driving force underneath and around the waters of the ship, leading, guiding and directing its path to this place, time and time again.

The Bible says in Proverbs 16 vs 9, *"In their hearts, humans plan their course, but the Lord establishes their steps."* (NIV) This was definitely true for the people making the decisions on Logos Hope, and I was about to be drastically changed, as here, in Subic Bay, I encountered a group of street teenage boys known in the Philippines as the "rugby boys."

CHAPTER ONE

The Bridge

Whenever I mention "the bridge," people assume I am speaking about the control centre of the Logos Hope. This is probably the most reasonable and logical assumption, considering that at the time of most of the discussions, I was living on-board the ship. Actually, the bridge I am referring to had nothing whatsoever to do with the ship. It was just a normal concrete bridge about one hundred metres long and ten metres wide. It was about a twenty-five-minute walk from the ship's berth at Rivera Wharf, Subic Bay Freeport Zone (SBFZ.) It was separated into three partitions by railings, and the middle partition was covered.

The bridge allowed most people to cross the dirty, polluted, and non-flowing Kalaklan River situated between SBFZ and Olongapo City. Olongapo is pronounced O-lon-gap-oh, not Apongalo or Opangola, or any of the other English variations I have heard that bear little or no resemblance to how it reads, let alone how it sounds! I highlight the fact that *most* people were allowed access to Olongapo via the bridge. There were numerous security guards checking identification at a specially placed guard station at the SBFZ end of the bridge twenty-four hours a day, seven days a week. I never saw them actually stop anyone from crossing, with the exception of the "rugby boys" that is, but then in the minds of the security officers and many local people, they don't count.

Fortunately, at the point that I was dying of boredom on the ship (as it was seemingly caught in some sort of time capsule, unable to conclude its dry dock repairs), some of the more enthusiastic crew members went hunting for a suitable location to begin some weekend street evangelism. They chose the bridge to set up a book table as it was an ideal location due to the quantity of people traffic flowing across it on a regular basis. It would also provide shelter from the rain as we entered the rainy season. On hearing of this project, I stopped whinging to Dan (the Personnel Manager on the ship) that I was bored and didn't have anything to do. I hightailed it down to the bridge every Saturday to be involved in the new ministry which combined two of my passions, evangelism and literature.

Our book table stocked the cheapest Christian books and local language Bibles from the Book-fair. We were authorised to give Bibles away for free if we had a good conversation or if someone really wanted one and couldn't afford it. Our primary goal was to engage people in conversation about Christianity, to share the Gospel with them and to offer to pray with them. We gained their attention by singing Christian songs and later through the men doing some preaching.

On the first Saturday (7th July 2012,) there were at least ten crew members involved, but after this the interest waned, as it often does with street evangelism. There was still a regular group of four or five of us that continued the ministry. Initially, permission was just given for Saturdays, but this was later increased to six days a week.

As we were now going to the bridge daily, we started to get to know the people that lived and worked in the vicinity. Our new friends included a blind man who had an incredible singing voice, that sometimes sang Christian songs and a lady that had been selling home cooked food on the bridge for over thirty years! We obtained permission from a local church to use their facilities to store our books and other items each day after an initial attempt to lug everything back and forth from the ship was abandoned. This was a handy arrangement, although one day when I asked a lady from the church if they had any "chairs" she disappeared to the store room for a while returning after ten minutes with a "Chess" set and handed it to me announcing "chess." The funny thing was that it hadn't seemed a somewhat bizarre request for me to have made of her in the first place, as she had gone straight away to find it!

Soon after starting the bridge ministry, I saw a large group of boys congregating in an area underneath and to the side of the bridge several times a day and sometimes remaining there for long periods of time. They were doing something in their group but I couldn't see what it was as they were about fifty-metres away from us. The boys were underneath a covered concrete area that ran at a ninety-degree angle to the bridge leading away from it. From my vantage point, on the bridge, I had a good view of their comings and goings although I couldn't yet see the detail of their activity. Sometimes the younger boys stood naked in a circle and there was a lot of shouting and noise emanating from the area. The boys looked like they were aged ten to twenty years old and there were about twenty of them in the group.

Not long after our arrival, some of the younger boys came to check us out. They had to scramble out from their place of residence, make their way along a pipe balanced precariously against a large wall, and then climb up and through a hole in a piece of board at the top of a fence. Then they could either walk around and join the common people in the covered walkway or use their preferred option, entering the restricted area running parallel to the covered area with just a wire fence separating the two partitions. The boys approached us from the other side of the fence in various stages of undress asking our names, ages, countries and what we were doing. We told them who we were and asked them some similar questions.

I put my hand through the fence towards them and they immediately grabbed it as if it was fascinating, looked at it and then began gently stroking my fingers. I wondered what on earth they were doing and then they softly whispered to each other "white white." They were talking about the flecks of white under my fingernails. I realised that it must be a novelty for them as they weren't used to seeing white people and that they weren't going to do anything too drastic.

At a later stage of our ministry, once we knew the boys a little better, they began stroking the legs of a white crew member in a similar fashion. He asked them to stop as he was afraid the locals might think he had paid them to do it. I thought it was a bit unlikely but he said: "Well, some people like some weird things!"

After a while, some of the boys said "swimming, swimming" in English. They then moved away from the fence and stripped off the remainder of their clothes. They climbed up the barriers on the edge of the bridge, which had obviously been erected to prevent people falling into the river. Many local people stopped to watch the spectacle and to take pictures. One by one the boys launched themselves into the filthy and shallow water less than ten metres below, shouting things excitedly to each other before climbing back up to repeat the process over and over again. The local people, although keen to watch, looked disgusted and annoyed and made comments reflecting their obvious distaste. Some of the taller boys hit the riverbed when they jumped in causing mud to surface with them. They didn't seem at all concerned and just laughed and continued shouting to each other. They were really joyful and happy, having a great time.

The security officers, obviously under pressure from the local people to do "something" about the lack of propriety in their city, headed down to engage the boys in conversation. However, the boys were not keen on being engaged and took off across the river swimming frantically and using various pieces of wood as floats and rafts. The officers, on seeing that they were fighting a losing battle and probably not really knowing what they would say to the boys in any event, soon gave up and moved away. Seeing that they were safe again, the boys came back to the riverbank, got out of the water, got dressed, and disappeared under the bridge.

Interestingly, when the boys were being chased, I found myself rooting for them. I was hoping they would make good their escape and not siding with the officials as I might have expected myself to, having been a police officer formerly. I could see that the officials were not acting out of care or concern for the boys and that their only intention was to punish them for their bad behaviour. This was my first proper contact with the "rugby boys."

CHAPTER TWO

The "Rugby Boys"

At various points over the next few days, I could see the boys in their hideout again, so I tried to work out what they were doing. They seemed to be holding plastic bags with something inside, which they were placing over their nose and inhaling from. This process was being repeated several times before the bags were placed into pockets or passed around amongst the group. Some of the boys appeared to be fighting imaginary characters further along the river bank, away from the bigger group. They were drawing invisible swords and crouching in fighting positions, then engaging in combat with the air. It gradually dawned on me that the bags must contain some type of substance that was making them hallucinate. The realisation brought sadness and disbelief as some of the boys looked like they must be really young and were likely unaware of the dangers of solvent abuse.

Another shocking thing was that, as mentioned already, there were police and security around at all times, due to the nearby guard station, but none of them did anything about the solvent abuse. The boys seemed almost to be invisible to them. Sometimes, they watched them as if they couldn't do anything about it or as if they weren't really seeing them. On a few occasions, after I realised that the children were inhaling solvents, I asked the guards to intervene. However, they didn't seem to know what to do and just made comments like "they are there every day" and "rugby boys" and "not from our province so no jurisdiction." I was pretty frustrated by their inadequacy and lack of real concern.

On returning to the ship that evening, I carried out some research (on Wikipedia,) into the substance which I had been told was a household glue called "Rugby." I was really upset by my findings. The "rugby boy" issue was a well-known problem in many areas of the Philippines and other third world countries. Children as young as five and six and living in poverty, sniffed the glue to stave off hunger pangs. The drug convinced the body that the child had eaten, dampening the pain of hunger. But, every time a child inhaled solvents it damaged their brain often irreversibly. Over time, the child would become addicted to the intoxicating smell of the drug and would sell everything they owned just to buy a small amount. Sometimes, as with harder drugs, the older boys sold the substance to others in order to make a small profit so that they could buy their personal supply. The procedure created more addicts and usually younger ones as the older boys had no qualms about selling to them. The ultimate result of long term abuse could be permanent brain damage, living in a vegetative state, coma, and even death.

I learned that it was mandatory for suppliers and distributors of Rugby and other commonly abused solvents, to add a substance to it prior to sale to change the smell, preventing the addiction. However, many distributors broke the law as they were making their living from selling it to the children. Some would even show the children how to cover up the bottle to make it look like something else. It was very cheap for the children to buy. The groups of addicts usually contained a range of ages. The older boys bought the substance and distributed it to the group, although they would never admit it for obvious reasons. When a child did manage to stop inhaling the solvents thereby breaking the addiction, their skin could continue to smell of it for up to a year as it seeped out gradually through their pores.

Naively, I at first thought that if only the boys could be told about the damage they were doing to their bodies and minds they would reconsider their lifestyle choice. I wanted to get information to them to educate them about the dangers of inhaling solvents as I believed it would really make a difference. However, later when we had a translator and I was finally able to communicate the dangers properly.

They collectively replied, "We already know" and from one boy, aged twelve, "I don't know why I'm still alive."

That was when it hit me that the boys didn't care. They didn't care about their lives or their futures or anything apart from the twenty-four hours in front of them. They didn't care whether they lived or died because their lives were intolerable and they were just trying to make it through each day. It took me a while to really accept the reality of the situation. It was just so alien to anything I had experienced before. When it finally sunk in, I was devastated by the realisation that the children had no hope and no plans for the future, they were just waiting to die.

Soon after that, we were at the bridge one day and the large group of boys was underneath as usual. This day, they were making more noise than usual, attracting my attention. Most of the younger boys were naked after swimming in the river and had gathered in a circle. I heard loud cries from one of the boys as if he was in real pain. The crying continued for about five minutes. I became really upset as I was convinced there was some type of serious assault occurring on one of the younger boys. I tried to forget the incident, but couldn't put it out of my mind and had to leave the bridge before the end of my shift.

Others told me that I needed to move past what I imagined might have happened. They said that the devil was trying to stop me from being involved in the evangelism on the bridge. But I couldn't accept that several of us had just stood there on the bridge hearing the boy crying and not doing anything about it. I kept thinking that had it been in England someone would have gone to investigate and put a stop to it. But in the Philippines the boys were invisible to most local people and so they just ignored them, besides making comments about "dirty rugby boys, always causing trouble" and the like. I prayed that God would help me to overcome my fears as I returned to the bridge the following day.

CHAPTER THREE

The Bridge Team

I regularly worked on the bridge with Nick from Georgia (not in America,) whom the boys called "Sir Nick" and Thabo from South Africa, whom they called "chocolate" because he is black. We tried to explain to them that they shouldn't call him that, but of course this just made them say it more often. I don't think children in the Philippines understand the concept of racism and, in any event, Thabo just thought it was funny. They called me "Ma'am Natalie" but pronounced all the syllables of my name separately with a lilt at the end "Na-taa-lcee." The "Ma'am" started off as a term of respect, but over time became more like "Mum," despite my frequent reminders that I was not.

Nick and Thabo both had a heart for the ministry and the three of us were a good team. We made an early decision that we would go to the bridge regardless of the weather conditions. At the start of our ministry the country was just entering its rainy season and this resulted in some crazy moments, particularly as we were trying to sell books. When I say "rainy season" I don't just mean a bit of rain, I'm talking about typhoons, floods and tropical winds that can materialise from nothing in a matter of minutes. In fact, predicting the weather became a minor competition as it was possible to spot a tiny grey cloud on the horizon one minute and then to be plunged into a typhoon within sixty seconds. We made a plastic sheet covering for our books and spent a lot of time covering and uncovering the book table. This makeshift cover was totally insufficient for the typhoon weather, and we (and our books) often got soaked because the bridge only had a small roof cover and was open to the elements on both sides. At these times, we waited until the weather had calmed down and then dried off in the sun after an hour or so.

I recall one day trying to shelter some kids, who were soaking wet, freezing cold and poorly clothed, inside my jacket and with an umbrella which was blowing around fiercely in the wind. It was possible to shout at the top of our voices, in the midst of this weather system and not be heard, so mostly we didn't try to communicate with each other. We just attached the single umbrella that we possessed to the metal railings near the ground and hid underneath it, sometimes being forced to hold on for dear life when the wind increased.

On another occasion, we were caught in a typhoon when trying to move all of our books in cardboard boxes stacked high on a trolley, which was really too heavy in the first place. The wind and heavy rain roared around Nick and Thabo, as they forced me to leave them struggling with the trolley, in an exposed area of the car-park. I took cover nearby and laughed a lot, along with the many local people watching, at the ridiculous situation they were in. The two of them finally made it to safety, completely drenched and windswept, but also laughing at what had been their predicament. We repeatedly returned to the ship soaked to the skin, but most of the time we were still cheerful and joking around.

Having spent more time in the Philippines and now knowing what typhoons can do, I am amazed at the risks that we took, but it didn't seem dangerous at the time. We just decided that people needed to hear the Gospel regardless of the weather, so we took it to them. The fact that on some days we were unable to talk to anyone, due to being forced to take cover for long spells, didn't really occur to us and we did have a lot of fun with the tropical weather. Some other ship crew members and many local people thought the three of us were really crazy, as we often didn't have umbrellas. The locals called out "Ma'am, ma'am, where's your umbrella? It's raining, can't you see?" in the middle of a typhoon, which I found hilarious.

In the Philippines, there were a number of superstitions relating to getting wet and umbrellas were considered an essential item. They were regularly being sold on the bridge, but on the day that I considered buying one, the unfortunate vendor's demonstration went badly wrong as he proudly and confidently pressed the button to open it up and immediately the metal spikes pierced the material all the way round. At least he saw the funny side as I determined *not* to buy one. Another time Nick accidentally hit a man fully in the face with one as he gesticulated wildly whilst telling a story. The man was really angry turning to Nick and warning "Next time….!" (as if Nick planned to do it again) in a threatening tone, as Nick offered his profuse apologies. Umbrellas were generally useless due to the tropical winds, in any event, and people that carried them spent more time fighting to keep them upright without them breaking, than being protected from the rain.

Early on in our bridge ministry, Nick and Thabo were learning to play the guitar. It was highly entertaining as their initial efforts were painful to listen to, especially when they also tried to sing together. People pulled faces as they walked past and I put my fingers in my ears. Neither of them could start the songs on the right note, or even in the right key, but if I helped them start with the right note it generally worked out okay. Once, when I came back from a lunch break I could see them singing from a distance so I braced myself as I got nearer. I briefly considered leaving again and returning later, but they actually sounded really good. I waited for them to finish at which point they both looked at me, awaiting the inevitable criticism, but I had nothing negative to say as it had sounded good. I think they had even surprised themselves.

Thankfully, they improved quickly after this so we began singing Christian songs to attract the attention of the boys under the bridge. We wanted to try and divert them away from their solvent abuse to something more wholesome. When they emerged, and began to listen, we taught them Christian songs including one in Tagalog (the main language in the Philippines and pronounced Ta-gaa-log.) Some of them already knew, *Kay Buti Buti Mo Panginoon*, which roughly translates as "the Lord is good." The younger boys joined in enthusiastically with the song and *Jesus Loves Me This I Know*, which a few of them knew from attendance at Sunday School as small children.

It made me sad to think that they were so immersed in drug abuse having attended Sunday School in the past.

Our activity's impact on the local people was immediately obvious. The boys were transformed from dirty, naked, drug-taking, river boys, swearing and fighting, to smiling boys, fully-clothed, singing Christian songs. A local lady working daily selling food on the bridge even gave each of us a penny sweet after one such performance and told the boys that their singing was beautiful.

The appearance of the guitar attracted some of the older boys including Matthew who was eighteen. He began to come to the bridge regularly for guitar lessons with Nick. He repeatedly played the lyrics *Here I am waiting, abide in me I pray, Here I am longing for you....* (Hillsong United.) Sometimes, when he was high on solvents, he drifted off and played the same part over and over again or got all of the notes wrong. But, at other times he played it reasonably well and the other boys gathered to listen. This made me feel emotional as the song was the story of Matthew's life. He had made a commitment to Jesus in the past and was still claiming to be a Christian, but he had had an ongoing battle with solvent addiction for years. We saw the struggle that he was having and it hurt to witness it and not be able to help him until he really wanted us to. His confident assertions about his faith were at times difficult for us due to the lifestyle he continued to live. But, I believe he was genuinely struggling with the issues he faced and wasn't deliberately succumbing to temptations as I saw his efforts to fight against them at times.

One day Matthew wrote "Jesus Loves You" on the arm of one of the youngest boys (whom we later discovered was Muslim.) He then explained to the younger boy what the phrase meant. It was a moving moment--the leaders are highly respected amongst the boys and the younger boy was hanging on his every word.

In Filipino culture, it is not embarrassing or shameful to be known as a Christian, even as a teenager. The country has Catholic roots so most people believe in God. Coming from England, it was at first a refreshing change for me. But I soon discovered that there were other challenges. For many people, faith in God had taken a backseat in their lives, being reduced to a formality, and a lot of the time there was no personal relationship with Jesus.

We had a large number of copies of *The Greatest Story Ever Told* in Tagalog. This was the story of Jesus told in colourful cartoon format for children. We encouraged the boys to read it and explained the story to them. But, their attention spans were not very long and frustratingly their friends often distracted them, encouraging them to go and play or take solvents. The older boys and the ones in the middle also kept their distance from us at first as they were trying to work out whether they could trust us. If we wanted to speak to them we asked for them by name and then they came out from their hide-out, found out what we wanted, and left again. They came to play the guitar, or if they had a reason to be there, but they didn't want to just hang around with us like the younger ones did as they had an element of street credibility to maintain.

Thabo had been a street kid himself, so he understood the boys. Maybe for this reason, he objected to them refusing to go to school and not even wanting to study. In South Africa, an education was considered a privilege. He often told the boys off for their attitudes. The boys acted as if they were listening but weren't really paying attention. Thabo also objected when the boys took their clothes off to swim and would instruct them to "Put your trousers on." He was so paranoid about them removing their clothes that he developed a habit of saying to them, "Don't take your trousers off, okay?" when they had just arrived and had no intention of doing so. It made me laugh a lot especially as the boys just looked so confused by the bizarre and irrelevant instruction.

Nick and Thabo began to buy bread and other food for the boys. I was wary having heard from someone that it wasn't always a good idea as it might make them dependent on us. Then, when we left with the ship, I was worried that they might starve. It was a genuine belief and I didn't want to cause them more harm than good. But, the others reminded me that God would look after them when we left and with time I realised that they were right. So, my resistance lessened and I sometimes also bought the boys food. However, I was a bit frustrated one day when I saw them feeding the bread we had bought them to the fish in the river. Their simple and innocent explanation, "The fishes are hungry too!"

Sometimes the boys bought soft drinks which the vendors placed in plastic bags for drinking through a straw so that they (the vendor) could keep and recycle the bottle or glass (a common practice in the Philippines.) But mostly the boys took the remains of the food and drink that people passing by were carrying by tugging on them until they let go. Most people let go rather than getting into a struggle and some people felt sorry for them and gave things willingly.

One of the annoying things the boys did constantly was to ask us for our water when we had just purchased a new bottle. We couldn't really say no as they acted as if they were dying of thirst. Then, the Bible verse inconveniently popped into my head about refusing to give someone water being the same as refusing to help Jesus. The problem was that sensibly we could only allow them to drink the remains when we had finished with the bottle due to the risk of disease. In the end, we resolved the dilemma by buying two bottles and giving them one to share. This was especially necessary when we had played games with them and they had been running around and were hot and dehydrated as we couldn't then refuse to give them water.

Most of the boys were smoking in addition to sniffing solvents. The street vendors sold the cigarettes individually from the packet which was another new concept. I didn't make too much fuss about the boys smoking because I was more concerned about the solvent abuse which occurred much more frequently with greater damage to their short-term health. Some might disagree with my stance, as the children were very young, but I knew that their other vices could be dealt with later if they left the street.

I am an ex-smoker and only gave up when my whole lifestyle totally changed when I became a Christian. I had resented criticism of my lifestyle choices as I didn't want people to judge me. I felt that if I told the boys off every time I saw them smoking it would create an unnecessary barrier at this stage so it wasn't my priority. Having said that, I made it clear I didn't like it, and we made them move away from our book-table when smoking, which most of the time they respected.

I knew that I was still holding back in some ways as I felt myself getting emotionally attached to the boys. I was worried about the impact, both for me and for them, when we inevitably left with the ship. This was exacerbated as we didn't know exactly when we were leaving since the dry dock work kept being extended. Thabo and Nick encouraged me to open my heart to really care for and love the boys. It took me a while to break down the hurdles of mental resistance and fear that had naturally built up. I eventually managed it and the result was life changing.

CHAPTER FOUR

The Leaders

After a while, I met the first girl attached to the group. Rachel, who was sixteen, may have been in a relationship with one of the older boys and sometimes appeared with them. She wasn't a street girl, she had a job and a house to go home to. I gave her a wristband after sharing the Gospel with her. It had the text "The Lord is my Shepherd" on it so I explained to her what the verse meant. I expected her to keep it and look after it as it was a gift from a foreigner, which normally would be cherished and valued.

In the Philippines, white foreigners are treated with great respect and admiration, sometimes to the point of embarrassment. Filipino females often used whitener and other products to try and make themselves whiter and therefore more Western. They don't realise that just as many Westerners are spending a lot of time and money sunbathing or using sunbeds in order to try to change their skin colour. Filipino's, especially the younger people, had totally unrealistic expectations of Western countries, imagining them as some kind of paradise, mostly due to the comparative wealth and things they had seen in movies or on the TV. I tried to put a dampener on their enthusiasm by explaining that my country had many problems and that it wasn't any more beautiful than the Philippines. I didn't want them to waste their time saving their money and pining for something that would disappoint. Actually, it was a case of the "grass always being greener on the other side." Filipino's have a lot of great things that Westerners sometimes miss out on; community spirit, close family relationships and respect for the elderly and authority figures being some of the obvious examples.

However, in relation to my gift to Rachel, the next day, Rachel's boyfriend Jacob was wearing the wristband. Jacob tended to annoy me because although he was seventeen, he kept trying to cuddle me. I told him not to, but he complained that the other boys did it. I said, "They are just children," as I pointed at the twelve year olds. "You are seventeen." He would often hang around all day irritating us by lying in our way as we tried to serve customers or he would take our books. He also hid his flip flops underneath something to beg from the passers-by, they would see he had no shoes on and feel sorry for him. Unfortunately, this was a tactic used by many of our boys, but it annoyed me more when Jacob did it because he was older, capable of working and should have known better. When I lost my patience, I told him to put his shoes on and to stop begging and misrepresenting himself. However, I also prayed with him and encouraged him to look for work.

During our first month, Jacob left the bridge, and I didn't see him again until a few months later, when I was walking in the city and I heard "Hey Ma'am Natalie." I looked up and saw Jacob standing on the back of a jeepney working as a conductor.

A jeepney is a metal bus without windows that serves as the local public transportation in the Philippines. My Dad affectionately labelled them as "rust buckets," after his first visit, which is probably quite accurate. Filipinos squash as many people as possible into the vehicles sometimes with additional people hanging illegally onto the back. Most Westerners are surprised to see that many jeepneys have large painted signs reading "Jesus Loves You" or "God is With Us" due to the Catholic roots of the country. They also have crosses and other religious artefacts hanging at the front of the vehicles. Quite a contrast to England where it's possible to get investigated, disciplined, and sacked for wearing a cross to work!

I spoke to Jacob briefly via Facebook, after I had seen him on the jeepney, and asked how he was doing but received no reply. Most of the boys have internet access through the internet cafes on a daily basis. It costs just fifteen pesos (about twenty pence) an hour.

The following day at the bridge there was a commotion as Jacob and Rachel arrived together in nice clean clothes. Jacob had clearly been solvent-free for some time. They walked straight past the other boys who were looking on in surprise and walked straight up to me. Jacob shook my hand and I told him it was good to see him. He nodded, smiled, and then immediately turned around with Rachel and left again. The other boys tried to approach them and talk to them, but Jacob waved them away from Rachel and the two of them then walked away, with a purposeful stride, as if they were gangsters or something. It was quite surreal, but I think Jacob was just responding to my Facebook message by showing me that they were doing well. I was pleased to see them.

One day, a large group of maybe ten or fifteen of the boys, including some of the older ones, came rushing towards us through the covered area on the bridge. The collection of boys was like some kind of tornado and they were all shouting and laughing! They reached our table and I was afraid for a minute that they would destroy everything or steal all of our books. There was nothing that we could have done due to the numbers of them versus us. But they just rushed around picking up books, looking at them, and putting them back down again. I tried desperately to remember some of the names from previous occasions. I failed in my efforts with the exception of one of the older boys who I knew was called David, he was twenty-one. I believed him to be one of the leaders of the group and I had seen a craziness in his eyes and behaviour that made me slightly afraid of him. I had also seen him present at the possible assault of the younger boy a few weeks earlier. The incident was still on my mind from time to time so I was wary of him.

David was at the centre of the tornado, whooping and shouting at us with nothing intelligible. He was obviously high on solvents as his eyes were glazed and unfocused. I didn't know what to do and felt pretty awkward, but I decided to try and say something to him as he was obviously the leader of the group on this day.

I looked into his eyes and said, "Jesus loves you, David." He looked back at me and for a second his face was serious. I saw he wanted to believe it. He said, "Jesus loves me?" and I said "Yes he does; he loves all of you." David then started shouting, "Jesus loves me, Jesus loves me" in a mocking way and all of the boys laughed. I felt a bit stupid and wasn't sure if I'd said the right thing. The tornado of boys then disappeared, leaving us dazed and confused.

The next time we saw David was during a clothing distribution. He was quiet and grateful for the clothes, saying "thank you" which was a nice surprise. He had also somehow acquired the wristband with the text "The Lord is my Shepherd "which I had given to Rachel and was wearing it around his ankle. I didn't understand how he had ended up with it but I knew by that point that things got passed around the group. I thought maybe he had taken it as he was one of the group leaders.

At one point, I bought wristbands for all of the boys and when David came to receive his I pointed down to his ankle at the one he had already acquired. I waited with some trepidation, expecting him to get really angry and demand his individual gift. Again, he surprised me when he simply smiled, said "okay," and left.

I saw David again when one of the younger boys was ill and we wanted to send him back to his family to recuperate. Although the boys were sleeping on the street many of them did have homes and families locally. They had run away or been forced to leave for a variety of reasons including abuse, neglect and poverty. Nick suggested we find one of the group leaders and advise them that we were sending the young boy home. We guessed that it might cause trouble for him later if he was involved in some sort of street fraternity and we just removed him from it. So, we went to find one of the leaders and happened upon David in the street. He was really friendly and helpful and said it was no problem for the boy to go home. I wondered how many more times he would say or do the unexpected, but I had noticed him softening towards us since the earlier encounter.

We didn't see David after that for a long time. Whenever I asked where he was his friends told me that he was working. I didn't really believe them as it sounded unrealistic. David had been in and out of rehab for his solvent abuse for many years and probably hadn't held a job for longer than a few weeks at a time. Also, when I asked the boys about individuals who were missing they would often tell me that this boy or that boy was "dead." They regularly mimed a slitting of the throat motion with their fingers before laughing when I looked shocked. Their information was not that reliable, especially when the "dead" boy turned up a few days later apparently having suffered no ill effects from the throat slitting. But, the information about David's whereabouts was consistent and it started to come from more reliable sources like Matthew and other leaders. So, eventually, I asked Matthew, "Is David really working and has he changed?" He just looked at me and quietly nodded.

I believed in my heart that something important had happened in David's life, but there was no confirmation for some time. One day, he contacted me on Facebook. After initial exchanges I said "God bless you" and he wrote "God is good, all the time" which I was surprised to see, and then "Ma'am Natalie…you save my life…..thanks" I tried to respond and get back in touch with him but he had logged off, so I had to wait for longer to find out what had actually happened. Shortly after this I had a proper online chat with him and he confirmed that he was working. He also said that he had realised that God loved him and had given his soul to God. I asked him if he was attending a church and he confirmed that he was going to a local Baptist Church—he named the pastor. I was so encouraged.

I only saw David once more near the bridge. He came over for literally five minutes to talk to someone else working on the bridge. I spoke to him briefly and shook his hand, but he said he had to leave as he was working so I couldn't really talk to him. I could see that he was solvent free and wearing clean clothes. The craziness had gone from his eyes and he had put on some weight. I think by this point he had realised the dangers of old temptations near to the bridge so I didn't really expect to see him again.

However, about six months later, I saw David walking in the city on his way to the mall. I barely recognised him as he was clean and wearing nice clothes. The biggest difference was definitely that his eyes were bright and cheerful and he was smiling during our whole conversation as he shook my hand. The drug-induced haze was nowhere to be seen and he confirmed that he was still working at the same job and continued to attend the church. It was indeed a miracle and I felt my heart soar as I continued my journey.

A considerable period of time later, I was saddened to hear from David's friends that he was drinking and abusing solvents again. His friends said they had also believed he had really changed as for a year or so his life was visibly different. Leaving this kind of lifestyle behind will not be easy for David and he will have temptations and trials that he may fall victim to along the way. His initial transformation was so drastic and seemed to occur almost independently of our bridge ministry. I believe he needed to know that someone loved him and cared about his life. I think when he realised that his life was significant and important to God this triggered the change. I hope and pray that it was a genuine miracle of the Holy Spirit in David's life and that he is truly born again and will turn back to God.

We encouraged all of the older boys to find work and had limited success from time to time. Sadly, though, most of the time they would work for a while and then lose their jobs and come back to hang around us again. It was always disappointing, but their lives and hearts hadn't really changed, only their temporal circumstances.

James, who was twenty, was an older boy who worked for longer periods of time, but always lost his job in the end. One day he came to the bridge carrying hot food that he was selling and smiling cheerfully. I purchased some food from him and was so happy to see the smile and the absence of drugs. I believed it was an answer to our prayer of only a few days before. A week later, James lost his job after a fight and was back with us looking downcast again, but we kept persevering and praying for him and the other boys.

The stories of some of the older boys provide a good example of the emotional ups and downs we faced on a daily basis when working with the boys. There was the excitement of seeing the initial changes, and then the disappointment of the failure, sometimes just a few days later. It really reminded us, that God had to do the work in the hearts of the boys, and that we couldn't accomplish anything life-changing in our own strength. "*Humanly speaking, it is impossible. But with God, all things are possible.*" Matthew 19 vs 26

CHAPTER FIVE

The Young Ones

I grew particularly close to some of the younger boys. Reuben, who was twelve, and Joshua, just ten. I couldn't stand to see them inhaling solvents because they were so young. Reuben wanted me to play games and run around with him. When he saw me coming down the street, he developed a habit of running towards me shouting, "Ma'am Natalie" and then jumping into my arms. He was small enough to do this, and very childlike in many respects even though he was twelve.

Sometimes he grabbed my hand shouting "Tara na!" which means "Let's go" and then started running along the bridge, dragging me with him. I responded, "Where are we going?" But there was no reply, he just liked to play games. He often put on my jacket and strapped on my rucksack, both of which were far too big for him, then paraded around with them on and had pictures taken. He brought a kitten to the bridge one day and spent all day playing with it. He didn't seem as interested in the solvents as the others and sometimes stayed with us all day without taking any. He just lay under our book table, sleeping or playing quietly. He could also be pretty funny and he joked around with us despite the language barrier.

The only boy coming regularly to the bridge but not inhaling solvents was Noah, who was nine. We discouraged him from hanging around with the group, but his mother was working nearby and, as the schooling hours in the Philippines were limited, he came in his free time. He was often bullied by the other boys who hit and pinched him, making him cry. The boys showed no mercy in this respect and little sympathy for each other's distresses unless they were serious. Noah kept us all entertained with his antics, hiding completely in a cardboard box and popping out suddenly or dancing on Thabo's feet as Nick played the guitar for them.

The boys frequently asked us for candy which could be bought on the bridge from the street vendors for one peso (just over a penny) each. Sometimes Noah bought two sweets keeping one for himself and giving one of us the other one. It was a nice gesture as he didn't really have any money and the other boys often bought cigarettes for one peso instead of buying candy and sharing it.

From time to time I saw another boy Malachi, who was also nine. He didn't appear to be using solvents (although that changed later.) He wasn't really part of our group of boys but just showed up occasionally. When I first saw him, he was sporting a black eye and had lifted his T-shirt up over his shaved head covering it completely so that only his face was visible. His arm was linked through a friends', and he was hobbling along with a limp, looking as if he was really ill and needed help. On talking to him, I found that he wasn't ill at all and that it was just a ploy whilst begging. I'm sure it worked because Malachi was very cute. Unfortunately, he also had a tendency to provoke the older boys into fights and once I had to spend an entire day trying to protect him from some of the older boys he had angered. He was clinging to the railing next to our table crying as the older boys kept trying to drag him away to hurt him in some way. Needless to say, I wouldn't let them. It was pathetic really as the boys were twice his age but were still intent on getting revenge for some, probably minor, misdemeanour.

Another day, I was sitting on the floor by the book table feeling a bit down when I heard a commotion followed by a host of small boy voices. I listened and could hear, "Natalie, Natalie, Natalie" over and over again. I waited for the boys to appear and then saw Nick with Reuben, Joshua, and Noah draped over his arms, excitedly jumping up and down. We had moved our table that day, due to the heat, so they hadn't known where we were. Nick just said, "Yes, yes. There she is!" and they ran over to me, immediately cheering me up with their obvious enthusiasm. Reuben and Joshua then fell asleep sitting on either side of me, leaning their heads on me, with my arms around their shoulders. But, I could smell the solvents on their breath and it made me especially sad because they were so young. I told Joshua that he would die if he continued this behaviour, but he just mocked me repeating, "You'll die" over and over again in a silly voice.

I tried to look after Joshua as he was the youngest boy addicted to solvents. I became aware that he was Muslim after a while, as he started saying, "No Jesus, no Jesus" whenever we spoke about Him. The others also confirmed he was Muslim. He became upset with me on one occasion and I didn't really know why due to the language barrier. He seemed to think I was upset with him as well and that there was a problem of some sort, but I didn't know what it was. Eventually, he threw a gift I had given him in the river whilst I was watching him. The other boys suggested it might be because he was Muslim and didn't like us talking about Jesus.

Later, Jude, a Filipino friend, stopped by and I finally had the translation necessary to work out what was wrong with Joshua and to share the Gospel properly with the other boys. Joshua told Jude that we were fighting and that we were angry with each other. I said that that wasn't the case and that I loved him and the other boys but that I was sad that he had thrown my gift in the river. Jude thought the misunderstanding was funny as it seemed a bit ridiculous that an adult female foreigner was "fighting" with a small boy. He told Joshua that we weren't fighting as I was his big sister. Joshua seemed surprised that I wasn't angry and then gave me a hug and it was all forgotten.

This incident is an example of the daily frustrations we faced at first due to not having any translation. I shared the Gospel with the boys through Jude and then prayed with them. All of the boys really listened and I believed afterwards that one of them may have sincerely trusted Jesus on this day, time would tell.

CHAPTER SIX

Department of Social Welfare and Development (DSWD)

The boys regularly came to see us and our book table, having established that we were not in any way linked with the local Department of Social Welfare and Development (DSWD.) They hated the organisation with a passion. Many of the boys had spent time in rehabilitation in Manila, (the capital city,) having been sent there by social workers from the DSWD. Some of them had been there several times but had just returned to the street upon being released. The general procedure was that every so often the DSWD had a campaign to catch all of the boys that they knew were sniffing solvents. They rounded them all up and took them to the hospital for a chest x-ray. They kept them for a few days and shaved their heads, resulting in them looking like gangsters, I assume for identification purposes. Then they released them back to the street pending the x-ray result.

If the x-ray showed that they had been inhaling solvents, the DSWD applied for a court order to send them to rehab for a minimum of eight months. If the boys arrived at the rehab part way through a school year (June-March) they had to remain for the entire year. The worst-case scenario, as one of our boys discovered, was that if they were captured in January or February, they would probably have to remain for the end of that school year and for the whole of the following year. Needless to say, the rehab centre, which was meant for adults, was not a popular place. Having visited the facility many times to date, I can now see why.

At first, I didn't really know anything about the DSWD. All of the information I had received was from the boys and there was obviously a strongly negative bias. To begin with we decided not to work in conjunction with the DSWD as it seemed to be the only way to build friendships with the boys. If they had thought we knew or were associating with their "enemies" they would not have come near us. I had never met the social workers and had no idea what their attitudes or working practices were like apart from the tales of the boys. I started subconsciously to dislike the organisation and think that they were just trying to cause trouble for the boys. Later, I learned that I was completely wrong and that many of the social workers had a deep love and concern for the boys as individuals and that they knew a lot about them. Some had even gone to the lengths of taking boys into their own homes to give them some respite from the street.

Nevertheless, I reassured the boys that we would not take them to DSWD or tell the agency their whereabouts. It did seem that the DSWD's practices were ineffective as many of the boys had already spent lengthy periods of time in rehab but they were still on the street. Others were repeatedly removed from the street only to be returned a few days later. On the occasions that we did cross paths with DSWD on the street, the boys ran away and the staff gave up looking for them almost immediately.

I think I was also influenced by one of the social workers that I met at City Hall in Olongapo one day. I went to see her as one of the boys had asked me to trace his birth mother and had given me his mother's details. However, the social worker didn't seem interested in helping at all and almost laughed at the request, saying that it would be impossible. I couldn't believe that she wasn't even willing to try, as it was such an important request. When she heard the name of the boy she recognised him as a "rugby boy" and began talking about rehab and a court order that was being processed. She almost seemed pleased, as if the judgement was some sort of achievement. With the enthusiastic assistance of her colleagues, she then spent the next half an hour running down the "rugby boys." She went on and on about how bad they were and that they were a blemish on society. I tried to keep my patience, but I didn't want to hear it. The speech confirmed my suspicions and the attitudes I had already seen in many local people. The boys were just a nuisance that, in the minds of the authorities, would be better off in another city.

CHAPTER SEVEN

Dentist to the Rescue

Our first medical incident, on 23rd August 2012, involved Mark, a sixteen-year-old boy that I hadn't seen before. I was working at the bridge book table as usual when my hand was grasped by Joel, twelve, who didn't say much but urgently dragged me to the side of the table a few metres away. He pointed to the ground and uttered one word, "crying."

I looked down and sure enough there was a boy lying curled up on the ground with his eyes closed and tears running down his cheeks. He had his hand pressed against his cheek and was clearly in pain. I knelt on the ground next to him and asked the other boys, who had by now gathered around the desperate figure, what his name was and what the problem was. They told me his name and that he had a toothache. I ascertained that he had been suffering for three months with no relief. I believed that he lived under the bridge with the other boys. I looked at him and felt the tears come to my eyes as I just felt so helpless and didn't know what to do. I told him I was going to pray for him and then did so.

I asked the others working with me what we could do, but they didn't have any ideas. Some were reluctant to get involved thinking it could open the floodgates for similar requests. I understood the point of view, looking at the big picture and all of the needs could easily be overwhelming. I was learning to combat this by dealing with one person and one situation at a time and trying to effectively help each individual where possible. I contacted a leader on the Logos Hope and asked if they could send one of their dentists to have a look at Mark.

Alternatively, I asked whether we could bring him to the ship for assistance. Unfortunately, both options were declined due to not having insurance to cover the situation. I began to feel desperate, knowing that I couldn't just leave Mark in this state. I told him to stay around the area and that I would find some way to help him. By this point, I was even thinking of taking him to the nearest dentist and shouldering the cost of treatment. The problem was that I was living on my ship allowance which was just twenty euros (a little over twelve pounds) a month and I thought this would be insufficient for even a basic check-up.

So, I went to lunch with Thabo. We were talking about Mark's sad situation and how hopeless it seemed to be. Suddenly, Thabo exclaimed "Oh, I know a Dentist." I replied "What? Where do they work?" Thabo said, "Here in Olongapo and she's a Christian." At that point I wasn't sure whether I was more excited that we might have a solution or more exasperated with Thabo for not having thought of it earlier. I stared at him incredulously as he continued by stating that he already had her number and could text the dentist straight away!

The obliging dentist immediately agreed to see Mark and dropped everything she was doing, including lunch with some friends, to rush back to her office. She prioritised responding to the urgent call of duty from her missionary friends, at least, that was what she posted on Facebook later. She even posted photos of her friends looking startled and her half-eaten lunch in the restaurant.

I then went to look for Mark to tell him of our success only to find that he had apparently vanished. I was so frustrated, having got this far only to find our patient missing! None of the boys were around, so I assumed he had gone off with them somewhere.

As a last resort, I decided to check under the bridge where the boys took their solvents every day. It was a bit of an intrusion, on principle we never went under the bridge so as to avoid invading their private space. They came to us when they wanted to and not the other way around. However, I decided to break with protocol considering that it was important. I climbed up over the wall and along the pipe next to the river peering down under the bridge as I did so. I couldn't see anything, I would actually have to go further into the dark area to check properly.

I was relieved when a local man appeared to assist me. He even came under the bridge for translation purposes just in case there was someone lurking there. It was really dark, damp and murky and knowing what had probably taken place there over the years gave me the creeps. But as I looked up I saw a lone boy curled up with his back to us right at the edge of the area. At first, I didn't think it was Mark, but when we called to him he turned over and I recognised him. I told him I needed to take him to the dentist. He seemed a bit confused as he had been sleeping, but he readily agreed to accompany us. We climbed back out of the darkness and back onto the bridge.

I told the rest of the bridge team that myself and Thabo were taking Mark to the dentist. They looked a bit surprised, but agreed to cover the book table alone allowing us to leave. We wandered through the town with Mark trailing behind us. He really looked a mess with his hair sticking up and his clothes dirty and torn. He was also extremely underweight, almost skeletal, and with bad acne from drug abuse. Many local people acknowledged him as he followed us and they seemed amused that we were accompanying him. He just kept his eyes down and plodded along behind us. I surmised from the local reactions that he too must be local rather than from a distant province as he had told us previously.

The Dentist was really friendly and helpful, and even found an extra T-shirt for Mark. She agreed to carry out the dental work for free, we could just pay for the painkillers. She extracted four of his teeth. I watched the operation thinking that in England, even at sixteen, my mum would probably have been there for this type of operation. I felt sad that no one seemed to care about Mark and he obviously wasn't capable of taking care of himself.

Actually, Mark's life was not at all how he presented it to us, but at this stage we didn't really know anything about him except that he was in pain and needed a dentist. Procedure concluded, we led Mark back through the town, buying some ice cream and other food which the dentist had recommended. We gave him the painkillers and then left the bridge for the day feeling somewhat satisfied that we had been able to help despite the initial barriers.

We didn't see Mark again for about a week. I kept asking the other boys where he was, but they just said he had gone home. I was surprised and asked them whether he had travelled for three hours to get home as this is how long he had told me it would take. I asked how he had got the money to make the trip. They didn't know and didn't really understand my questions. A week later, Mark reappeared, his teeth were still hurting but he was a lot better than before. He was very high on solvents though, which upset me as he seemed to be taking more than the others and always looked unhappy.

One day, on the bridge, I heard "Ma'am Natalie" behind me and turned to see a horrible evil faced mask on the face of someone walking towards me. The person's arms were outstretched as if they were a zombie in a movie. I pulled the mask off and it was Mark. He was really high and the mask had really frightened me. I told him not to wear the mask as it was evil. I really hated to see the boys like that. I regularly told them about the dangers of the drugs, but they didn't care and wouldn't listen.

CHAPTER EIGHT

Consolidating the Friendships

Over time, as we turned up for our daily ministry, the boys began communicating more frequently and asking us questions. We, in turn, asked for their basic details and most importantly where they were from, hoping to find out about their families. All of them told us that they were from far away provinces three or four hours minimum travelling time from Olongapo City. Most of them also said that their parents had died and that they had no family or relatives. I recall seeing the throat slitting motion with the hand and the word "patay" which means "dead" many times when asking about relatives, which mostly turned out later to be untrue. The few that admitted having family said that they had been thrown out of their houses or had run away due to physical abuse. Some even said that they would go home if they had the money to get there. They all claimed not to have attended school for a very long time. I was surprised by what they said, but didn't know the culture enough to question their statements at this stage.

Sometimes the boys swam in the river holding the plastic bags to their faces and inhaling the solvents at the same time. They made no attempt to disguise what they were doing from the local people who could clearly see from the bridge. When they appeared on the bridge itself, they were often high on solvents which we recognised by their glazed eyes, their extra confidence, the smell of the solvents, and sometimes even the trails of glue in their hair and on their faces. As I was getting to know the boys as individuals, I began to really hate the substance and the sight and smell of it, knowing the irreversible damage it was doing to their minds and bodies. Occasionally I thought of England and how open solvent abuse amongst children of their age just wouldn't be tolerated. I knew that most adults would have intervened, but we were a long way from England and attitudes and priorities were very different.

I became really attached to the boys and looked forward to seeing them every day. I had learnt their names and asked for their whereabouts if a boy was missing on a given day. We bought them basic food on most days, when we could afford it. I often took them to the street food stand around the corner and bought them rice for eight pesos (eleven pence) and some chicken to share. It was pretty funny as they all jumped on me hanging off my arms with one of them jumping on my back for a "piggyback." We probably looked a strange sight as we headed for the rice stand. Some local people still gave us looks of disgust, but I could see that attitudes were changing slowly and some people were silently encouraging our ministry to the boys.

Unfortunately, I always had to tell the boys off during the piggybacks. Whenever one boy jumped up another boy tried to do something to him which in England would be considered a sexual assault. I told the boys that it was wrong, but they just laughed as they knew I had been a police officer. I always stopped them from doing it, when I caught them. The eventual end result of the reinforcement was that when one of them tried to commit the crime, another would say "no....sexual assault....police!" They would then give a dramatic demonstration of someone being arrested and taken away in handcuffs. I think they got the point. They also frequently started singing *Gangnam Style* and doing the dance. In response because I didn't want to endorse the song lyrics, I said, "Hey, there's no sexy ladies around here" which normally stopped them in their tracks as they thought it was funny.

When one of the boys turned up with a bicycle, I didn't have time to wonder where it had come from as they ushered me onto the bike and I immediately took off with one of the boys on the back. I cycled, at high speed, about one hundred metres into the high street before realising that I wasn't really in control. I hadn't ridden a bike for a very long time and the passenger on the back was making things more unstable. I turned around and wobbled back only to be confronted by Nick. His face was a picture of worry mixed with annoyance. He demanded to know what on earth I had been thinking pointing out that the street was dangerous and there was a lot of traffic. I explained that I hadn't really been thinking at all as I had been caught up in the excitement of the moment. Sometimes, I forgot what others might think of me and got carried along with the activities and energies of the boys as they played. They were delighted of course because I was normally quite serious and telling them off for various misdemeanours.

My parents visited me in October 2012 and tried to take me to a beach somewhere, but I missed the boys and wondered if they were okay. Whilst walking around with my mum in the city, we saw Adam, who I thought was eleven, asleep on a large pipe ten metres above the river. My mum was worried he would fall off onto the rocks below if he moved in his sleep, but I had seen others sleeping here before so I reassured her. Then I saw the rest of the boys swimming in the river and when Simon, who was twelve, saw me, he shouted from the river "Ma'am Natalie, I miss you!" as I had been gone for a few days.

I satisfied my desire to spend time with the boys by taking my parents to the bridge for a few hours to meet them. They kept asking my mum and dad for their names and ages and then repeating them out loud over and over again whilst pointing at them. They weren't aware that it is quite rude to point at someone and to discuss their age, and my parents didn't mind. The boys then acquired water pistols and squirted us until one of them accidentally got my mum. He looked embarrassed and seemed to be preparing mentally for the shame of being told off, but the real shock came when my mum got the water pistol and squirted him back—I will never forget the expression on his face!

The next day, my parents told me that on the way back to their hotel, they had been approached by a young boy who they thought they might have met earlier with me. He just smiled and said, "Natalie is my mummy," and my mum didn't have the heart to correct him. I knew who the boy was because his family lived on the Subic Bay side of the bridge. He wasn't part of our regular group and wasn't abusing solvents. I often saw him wandering around collecting plastic recyclables in a large bag. When I had first met him, he had been with his cousin and I had shown them an Evangecube which we sometimes used to share the Gospel. When he saw Jesus on the cross he started crying and later when he left he shouted at the top of his voice "Jesus loves me!" over and over again.

CHAPTER NINE

Practical Help

I tried to think of other ways to help the boys as they constantly asked us for food, clothes, and money. We refused to give them money as it could so easily be used to buy solvents. What we didn't realise initially is that most things were easily saleable on the street in the Philippines. The boy's clothes were always ripped, torn and dirty and they "washed" them in the dirty river. They tried to persuade us to give them ten pesos (fourteen pence) for a shower but as we couldn't guarantee where the money was going, we declined. We later learned that the boys deliberately ripped their clothes to let the air in as it was hot. They wore long baggy T-shirts down to their knees and made belts for their shorts out of anything lying around. Sometimes their shorts developed big holes and became indecent, at which point we insisted on buying new ones for them.

I asked the ship leaders whether we could give the boys any clothing. The book-fair manager suggested we could use some old book-fair uniforms which happened to be the same as the uniform we were wearing to the bridge every day. I took a whole load of the T-shirts, which were maroon with a Logos Hope logo on them and the shorts and trousers which were beige. The boys came immediately to the fence area when they saw I had something to give them and started trying them on. There was some bickering requiring intervention as I tried to make sure the clothes were evenly distributed.

A few minutes after the boys had departed to show off their acquisitions, the local police appeared to ask if we had been robbed as they had seen the boys wearing our clothes. A lady police officer expressed sympathy for the boys and advised me that she was trying to find some space for them in an orphanage. I didn't say anything but thought to myself

"Good luck keeping them there." I knew the boys wouldn't stay anywhere they didn't want to. Some of them had already run away from some Christian homes with good reputations in the area.

The boys looked really smart as they paraded around in their new uniforms. I watched them coming and going and walking in a line back and forth along the pipe leading under the bridge. It was really quite funny to see and the locals were also amused. A few hours after the distribution, Nick, who was on his day off, came running up to me looking a bit angry and confused. He said, "I just ran into some of the boys wearing book-fair uniforms!" He had questioned them asking, "Where did you get these? Did you steal them?" And the boys had given the standard response to a foreigner when they don't understand, "Yes." I started laughing and provided a hasty explanation, apologising for forgetting to tell the rest of the team who hadn't all been working when I had had the idea.

I also bought the boys wristbands that read "The Lord is my Shepherd" and presented them to each of the boys in turn. I explained that whenever they read the verse they should remember that Jesus was watching over them and looking after them and that they could pray to Him anytime they wanted. They lined up eagerly, and in a somewhat more orderly fashion than the earlier clothing rabble, to receive the bands. They wore them proudly around their ankles. I had written their names on them and also made a list of the boys with their names and ages. I asked ship crew members to sign up to pray for each boy individually and sent an email with a similar request to England. I tried to email people with updates about their individual boys to keep them interested and praying.

The boys liked being treated as individuals, which was why learning their names had been so important and really helped us to connect with them. The wrist (or ankle) bands gradually disappeared in the following days. Some of the boys kept them for longer periods and all of them asked us for new ones whether they had one already or not. I learnt that no matter what we gave them they always asked for more. Yet it wasn't always that they wanted the thing they were asking for, they just wanted to see if we would give it to them, so we had to be disciplined in saying "no" at times.

We also gave them hoodies which we obtained from the ship because we knew they were sleeping on the street. These should have been helpful in keeping the noise out and more comfortable than cardboard boxes. But these, and the book-fair uniforms, also disappeared over time. Eventually we asked one of the older boys what was going on. He openly told us that all of the clothes were being sold. I asked another boy why they had done this and he just said, "We didn't need them." Sometimes what we thought they needed was very wrong. I was so desperate to help the boys that I was forgetting that it couldn't always be done in material ways. I started thinking, "How much money will it take to get these boys off the street and off drugs?", but I was convicted by the Bible passage in Psalm 49 vs 7-9:

"No one can redeem the life of another or give to God a ransom for them—the ransom for a life is costly, no payment is ever enough—so that they should live on forever and not see decay."

I read these verses twice in separate places shortly after I began thinking in material terms. However, the experiences that appeared outwardly negative or a waste of resources were good for us. We could see what was helpful and what wasn't, and it was only through our mistakes that we learnt.

My own clothes from the ship started to deteriorate due to the bridge work. Instead of replacing them, I used the holes to deal with the boys' demands. When they said, "Ma'am Natalie, give me T-shirt." I replied "No, you give me T-shirt!" pointing to the holes in my clothes. They laughed and didn't ask me again. As already mentioned, sometimes they weren't interested in getting the items. They wanted to test our care for them and they saw this in monetary terms. We had to learn to understand this and to be wise when spending money.

CHAPTER TEN

Internet Access and Social Media

As I briefly mentioned earlier, another thing that surprised us is that the boys all had access to the internet and all had Facebook accounts. They spent a large amount of their time online after begging in the street to get the money. The internet was pretty cheap and they liked to play computer games online. Sometimes, they played the games all night as some internet cafés were open twenty-four-seven.

Internet addiction was a big problem in the Philippines with large numbers of children spending most of their free time in the internet cafés. They could surf online virtually unmonitored for as long as they wanted. This was a particular problem during their school holidays as there weren't too many alternative options. Many parents were working long hours just to put food on the table. I even witnessed young boys watching a pornographic video in the middle of the day in one of the cafés. It was only switched off when I notified the manager who obliged but didn't seem unduly concerned. Some, but not all, of the cafés banned children from entering during school hours. Violent and addictive videos games like *Defence of the Ancients (DOTA)* and *World of Warcraft* were visible on nearly every screen on entry to the cafés. Children eagerly line up to wait for their turn.

I first learned that our younger street boys had internet access when I was walking along the street one day. Suddenly, three of the boys appeared as if by magic in front of me looking sheepish. They had descended a staircase and stepped out into the street directly in my path. I asked them what they were doing as they huddled together as if they had been caught in the act. They looked extremely suspicious so I was surprised when all they said was, "Internet café ma'am." I was a bit taken aback as I had believed that they didn't have enough money to eat. However, it was becoming evident that they felt they had sufficient to waste what they did have in the internet café. I was yet to learn that things were not always as they seemed in this respect.

This is an aspect of life in a third world country that a lot of people in the UK have asked me about. I will try to explain why they wasted potentially life-saving money like this. It is best illustrated in this way: one day Joel whilst begging, received one thousand pesos (about fourteen pounds) from a foreigner. This is a lot of money for an adult, who might earn just two hundred pesos a day as a security guard, let alone a child. A street meal could cost as little as thirty pesos. Joel returned to the group triumphantly waving his riches. I thought to myself, "Great, now we won't have to feed them for a week and then maybe some of them won't take drugs either." Wrong! Just a few minutes later Joel excitedly went into the city with a few of the other boys and returned an hour later with several fake guns. The money had gone. Joel hadn't even thought about buying food for that day, let alone future days or weeks.

These were young boys that hadn't been taught money management skills. They hadn't had access to toys or other material things. If they acquired money, whatever the source, they immediately bought toys or games, or spent it on computer games on the internet. It was guaranteed. The thought of saving the money for food isn't exciting for a teenage boy, but impressing his friends with the latest gadget definitely is. Food wasn't even a consideration until it became a necessity when they recognised that unless they ate they would collapse. It's sad, but the boys knew that they could stave off the hunger pangs with solvents later on and that it was cheaper than buying food, so this is what they did. They honestly didn't think about anything except the next few hours in front of them. They had no plans and no future. Part of the reason was that they had become invisible to people and they were just crying out for attention. They were crying out for someone to notice them. They wanted someone to take an interest in them as individuals, to spend time with them, to really get to know them and not then to disappear from their lives. They needed, as we all do, to matter to someone, to be cared for and loved by someone.

CHAPTER ELEVEN

Living at the Hospital

Inevitably, spending a lot of time with the boys every day resulted in us having to deal with various medical incidents that cropped up. The system in the Philippines was that a person could only receive treatment at the hospital if they could pay for it, even in an emergency. Clearly, the boys were never going to be in a position to pay for any type of treatment. Often the security guards at the entrance to the hospital wouldn't even let them in through the front door, let alone establish what was wrong with them or whether it was urgent. It was just another example of how the children had become invisible to local people. They were seen by those in authority as a nuisance or a shame for society to be embarrassed about and no one really knew what to do with them. I think the authorities wished they weren't there and would go somewhere else. It was a bit like the police in England who sometimes moved homeless people on from one town to another, which didn't deal with the root of the problem.

It was a real blessing to have the Christian charity *Helping Hands Healing Hearts* stationed within the local hospital, which itself was only a five-minute walk from the bridge. Amongst other things, the charity helped financially if a person couldn't afford treatment. We often went begging to their office with one of our boys in tow to ask for help. They knew all of the boys we took to them from previous incidents. They often also knew where they lived and things about their lives. On speaking with the staff, I again became suspicious of the stories the boys had told us about their family backgrounds. They were clearly local to the area, although they had told us they lived a long way away in Manila and other far off lands!

Sometimes, we felt as if we were living at the hospital as we were so frequently in attendance. The problem was that if we had to take one boy then others mysteriously developed illnesses or cuts and scrapes that hadn't been a problem to them before that, in their view, suddenly needed attention. We ended up taking a herd of them all together which caused further problems as they fought and jostled with each other in the waiting area or disappeared outside to smoke when their name was being called.

In the early days, one of our regular boys Solomon developed a high fever. We were alerted to this by Joel, the same boy that had grabbed my hand and dragged me to Mark. He knew that we would help if we could. Solomon was lying on the floor and was very hot. Again, I prayed for him and didn't really know what else to do. Joel was crying as he said he didn't want Solomon to die. I told him that he wouldn't die, but I didn't really know what would happen as I thought he might have contracted some kind of disease from the river as it was polluted. We let him rest for a few hours and kept an eye on him, but his temperature wasn't going down and he was becoming less coherent. So, Nick and I took him to the hospital.

We sat for hours waiting for various tests and eventually decided to visit *Helping Hands* who immediately offered to help us with the cost of the medicine. They also knew Solomon already and told us that he lived locally in a poorer part of town in a mountainous area. He had eight siblings and the family didn't have enough food. On hearing his history being discussed, Solomon then admitted that he had originally run away to find food and had stayed on the street when he got involved with the "rugby boys." He agreed to go home for one week to recover from the fever. He was given antibiotics and we took him for a meal afterwards. However, even this was not straightforward because as soon as the other boys saw us back in the street they wanted to accompany us for the meal. As we had little money and didn't want to start a trend, we advised them that it was a special treat for Solomon because he was sick and that he would be going home afterwards to rest. They were all really concerned about him and accepted what we said, which was a relief.

After the meal, we put Solomon into a jeepney and made sure he knew how to take his medicine. He still had a fever and we worried about sending him home alone when we didn't know what sort of reception he would get. But, it was impossible for us to accompany him at this time of the evening without knowing where to go or how to get back, so we prayed for him instead. He promised that he would stay at home for at least a week to recover. We spent a lot of time telling him about Jesus and encouraging him to go back to school. We were hoping we wouldn't see him again on the bridge.

Unfortunately, on arrival the next day, there was Solomon's cheeky face grinning at us. I went straight over to him and demanded to know, "What are you doing here?" but he just grinned as if it was fine and the other boys also were laughing. At least he no longer had a temperature and seemed to have recovered. But then I saw that his medicine bottle was empty and the tablets had gone. They were meant to have lasted for a whole week! He indicated that all of the other boys had shared them with him. I suddenly realised how dangerous it had been to give a group of boys already experimenting with drugs any type of medicine, expecting them to take it properly. Learning from the experience, on the next occasion, we kept the medicine ourselves and gave it to the boys as necessary. Shortly after that, however, Solomon disappeared from the bridge never to return, and his friends advised that he had gone back to school.

Another accident, which I didn't really want to deal with directly, occurred under the bridge. One of the boys came running, shouting "Accident! Accident!" I went to have a look and could see that Joel had fallen and that his bone was partially protruding from a gash on his ankle area. I couldn't deal with it and knew I didn't have to as there were other people working with me. Nick helped Joel to the hospital where the doctor said that it was just as well someone had brought him or there may have been a serious infection with dire consequences.

The wound required ongoing treatment, ideally daily at the hospital, but we knew that there was no way Joel was responsible enough to attend a daily appointment. To deal with the situation, now that we were self-appointed medical experts, we purchased very basic supplies of alcohol, cotton wool, bandages, and some kind of antiseptic cream. Then we told Joel that he had to come and see us every day to get the dressing changed. We did this every day for a week and were grateful when, another crew member from Logos Hope, saw us attending to him on the bridge and was so moved that he offered to pay for any additional medicine. Our actions also raised the attention of the passers-by who looked shocked to see white foreigners sitting on the dirty ground taking time and care to clean the wound of a street boy. The wound began to heal, but due to the conditions on the street and Joel running around it got infected and we had to take him back to the hospital.

Eventually, to my relief, our frequent cleaning, changing dressings, and prayer paid off and the wound healed. I was really relieved as I hadn't a clue what I was doing but had to pretend to the boys that I did, otherwise, they wouldn't have trusted me to help Joel. Without intervention, he wouldn't have had any treatment, which could have resulted in serious consequences, like losing his foot!

The boys started calling me "Doctor." As I mentioned before, the boys didn't think beyond twenty-four hours ahead as evidenced by their solvent use. I was constantly afraid that Joel would tire of the treatment and say that he had had enough, it was obviously painful for him. However, to his credit, he must've realised that it was serious and decided to be sensible. We also used the medical kit to deal with many cuts and scrapes. The boys liked to feel that they had some injury or other problem worthy of our attention. Even Matthew the leader asked me to attend to a minor injury. I used a cotton bud to clean the wounds with alcohol, then stuck some cream in it and put a bandage or band aid over the top. Simples!

CHAPTER TWELVE

Breaches of Trust

One of the surprises for me when working with the boys was that we hadn't had any major problems with thieving. We didn't want to put temptation in their path, but we also didn't want to have to watch over our belongings all of the time. So we trusted the boys that we knew not to go in our bags and not to take things from us. We had a few instances of theft which stand out in my mind, as it was always upsetting due to the breach of trust rather than the value of the items.

We were selling bracelets with Bible verses on them from the book table, and a few of these disappeared one day. Unfortunately, it happened at the same time that some men from one of the local children's homes had come to see our ministry on the bridge. I got upset and angry with the boys. The men had come to see whether any of the boys might be suitable for one of the homes but left shortly after the theft, advising me to be patient with the boys. Before the theft, I had already been a bit disappointed by the visit of the men. One of the older visitors had commented, "What these boys need is a bit of stick!" demonstrating a thrashing motion with his hand. Some of our older boys overheard the comment, and understanding, they turned their heads away in disgust. I thought, "That is the last thing they need. They have experienced enough of that at home which is why many of them are here." We had spent a lot of time working with the boys, preparing them to leave the street and the progress could have been destroyed with one careless comment.

The bracelets were later returned, broken, by a boy who hadn't taken them. He said very politely, "Are you missing these ma'am?" as he held them out to me. I was reassured, as I realised, that the damage could have been caused by accident and that at least they hadn't been sold. The boys hadn't been taught how to look after things, so sometimes damaged them unintentionally, by handling them roughly without due consideration of the consequences. Or by fighting with each other for possession!

We did experience a theft by one of our own boys and it really hurt me. The incident started when I caught Reuben red-handed. He was going through my purse which someone had removed from my bag, which had been underneath the book table. I saw him take two pesos (three pence) out of it and I immediately challenged him and told him to give the money back. He refused and ran off with the coins laughing and taunting me. Basically, his view was that it was just two pesos and it didn't matter. But, I couldn't allow him to get away with it, I had to make the point that stealing even a small amount of money is wrong. I double checked my purse and then, to my dismay, saw that another five hundred pesos (seven pounds) was missing. I was ninety percent sure that the money had been there although I would rather have believed I had made a mistake. I went after Reuben and challenged him about the additional funds. He became very upset and promptly gave the two pesos back.

A local man intervened on my behalf and also accused Reuben of taking the money. He continued to deny it and started crying and walking around mumbling to himself and getting really upset and angry. By this point, I could see by his reaction that he hadn't taken the money so I asked the local man to ask him who was responsible. He said he didn't know.

I was upset by this point as I was hurt by the breach of trust. I went and sat away from everyone to think about what had happened and who might have taken the money. Another local man saw that I was upset and tried to find out what had happened. He dragged one of the sleeping boys, Luke, aged fifteen, out from under our table and started violently beating him around the head. I was distraught as I attempted to intervene and protect Luke. I knew he wasn't responsible because he had been asleep! I couldn't believe the level of violence the man was using on an innocent child supposedly on my behalf. Luke was crying and shouting at the man through angry tears as I tried to calm the situation down.

One of the other boys came over to me. He took my hand and informed me that they had reported the theft to the police and that I needed to go and talk to the police officer. I didn't really want to as I was upset but I knew it must've been hard for the boys to approach the police. Since the officers were waiting I went to see them. The boys gathered around and I could see that some of them were as upset as I was. They were all shaking their heads and looking ashamed on behalf of their group. I noticed that one boy was missing, Joshua. When I thought about it, I knew he was the culprit, he had left in a hurry a little earlier with no explanation. The boys were all very apologetic. I told the police that I didn't want to file a complaint but that I was hurt by the breach of trust.

I didn't go to the bridge the following day. It was one of the few occasions when I couldn't face the boys. I asked Thabo to challenge them and to see if he could recover my money and get to the bottom of the matter.

On his return, he said that they had been very subdued and that there had been no visible solvent abuse all day. They were very keen to sing the songs and to behave themselves. This was interesting as it proved to some extent that the boys weren't so addicted to the solvents that they had to take them every day. Thabo talked to Joshua about the incident, but he didn't admit anything. I went back the next day and Joshua wasn't around. In fact, I didn't see him for two weeks. I asked his friends where he was and they said that he was at home. I thought maybe his relatives had found out what had happened and were angry with him for thieving. I couldn't have been more wrong!

After a while, one of the boys told me that Joshua had decided to give the money back to me as he had felt so guilty about it. However, on finding out about the money and Joshua's intention to return it, his uncle had taken it and told him that if he tried to return it to me he would kill him! At this stage, I thought things were getting a little out of control. I told the messenger to advise Joshua that if he came and said sorry to me in person that would be the end of the matter. I asked the boy why Joshua had stolen the money and was casually informed, "You didn't need it." Actually, I had needed it, as it was nearly half of my pocket money for the whole month. The boys saw us handling book-fair money at the book table and often thought we had more personal money than we did.

Over time, I had become friends with all of the boys on Facebook and they often contacted me online when I wasn't at the bridge to ask where I was. Joshua sent me a message apologising for stealing the money. I accepted the apology but said that I still wanted to see and talk to him in person.

A few days after receiving the message, when I got to the bridge, I saw a small figure standing further along the bridge. The figure had a T-shirt pulled completely up over their head so I couldn't see who it was. I thought it might be Joshua so I called out to him. He peeked at me quickly through a gap in the clothing and then ran away to the other side of the fence where all the other boys were still sleeping. I decided to give him time so I carried on setting up the table. But, I was distracted because out of the corner of my eye, I kept seeing him looking at me through gaps in his clothes. I told one of the other older boys to tell him to come and say sorry to me and that it would be okay. I could see he was finding it very hard—he had probably never been asked to apologise for anything in his life. He came nearer and nearer to the fence and I moved over to talk to him, but he kept backing away. Eventually, he removed his T-shirt a little but still didn't say anything. I touched his head through the fence and said to him that he should look at me and say he was sorry. After a while, he complied and I said it was okay and gave him a hug. I didn't want to make a big thing of it so I went back to what I was doing. A few minutes later I looked over and saw that he was crying quietly by himself. The incident damaged my relationship with Joshua, and although I tried, I found it difficult to go back to how we had been before.

The final theft incident occurred a lot later in our ministry. Our bridge team had changed and there were some new crew members with me. Some new boys came that I hadn't seen before. I didn't pay them much attention as we were used to having extra boys and they seemed to know our other boys. However, after a while, I noticed one of them blatantly going through the bag of one of the crew members, seemingly making no attempt to hide what he was doing. I shouted at him and made all of the boys stay where they were whilst we checked their pockets. I was really angry, but as they didn't seem to have anything on them, and the crew members couldn't confirm that anything had been taken, we had to let them go. I think they hid the money in their underwear because some of them even pulled their shorts down to prove they weren't hiding anything and probably to protest about the accusation! Immediately after the search, the new boys ran off.

Shortly after they had gone, a crew member found that she had lost some foreign currency and some local money. Our regular boys also disappeared and, a short time later, one of them came running back to say that one of the thieves had been found and some of the money recovered. I heard a loud commotion in the street and went over to see what was going on. I saw a local man who looked pretty angry holding a boy of about thirteen by the scruff of his neck. The man said to me "Have you lost something?" and I explained what had happened. He told me that the boy had tried to present the foreign currency in his store. A large group had gathered including all of our regular boys, so I took the opportunity to show mercy to the child. I asked the man to translate then asked the boy if he was sorry. When he said yes, I advised him that we forgave him and then I told him and all the onlookers about Jesus, and how He has forgiven our sins allowing us to forgive others when they sin against us. It was really a great opportunity for our boys to see us put our words into practice.

Unfortunately, the new crew members were so shocked by what they had witnessed that they were reluctant to come back to the bridge. I explained that it wasn't our regular boys, but I think they had been horrified by some of the behaviour and by seeing me upset when I was meant to be in charge. One female crew member said that the boys had repeatedly asked her if she had a boyfriend. They then tried to cuddle her and had been jumping all over her. She believed they were trying to assault her or touch her inappropriately.

Actually, our regular boys were always careful with us, as females, in this respect. There was a lot of messing around and physical contact between us and the boys, but they always made efforts not to make us uncomfortable, by keeping their hands to themselves. They didn't take advantage of the freedom that we allowed them when playing games and other rough and tumble. I knew that the boys were just curious about foreigners and their white skin and different features, hence the many questions and comments. It was how they expressed their curiosity because they felt comfortable with us, so it didn't bother me, but I had to appreciate that others were different and that the boy's behaviour could be misinterpreted.

I was glad that the other crew members hadn't been there when our regular boys were behaving really badly, which they did on occasion. It tended to be bad behaviour as a group as they riled each other up. They begged from the customers browsing at the book table or hid under the table which had a cover hanging down. Then they snatched half eaten food or drinks that people had in their hands whilst looking at the books, making them jump back in shock as they hadn't even known anybody was there. Actually, that was quite funny, but we dutifully told them off until one day when we didn't need to. On that memorable day, a local man became irate when they chose him as their target. He dragged two of the boys out from under the table shouting and threatening to beat them in the street. We just looked the other way and whistled, as we had been expecting something like this for a while. The boys had to learn to behave themselves.

CHAPTER THIRTEEN

Gang Fight and Other Trouble

People often told me that my police background had prepared me for working with the street boys. At the time, I couldn't see it, but as I write I can see that maybe I might have been less intimidated by the boys due to my previous line of work. The difference was that in the police you didn't tend to be emotionally involved with the people you were dealing with. Sometimes, I dealt with cases where a relationship was developed with a victim or witness due to preparation for a court case. Then, it was hard if the result was not what had been hoped for. But working with the boys was so much more challenging because it was impossible not to get emotionally involved due to the length of time that we were working with them for. In most cases, they didn't have anyone else that really loved or cared for them. They grew to love and trust me, but they were physically damaging themselves every day right in front of me and I was powerless to stop it. The problem is that we had become involved in long-term work without resources or partnerships to adequately support us. It wasn't anybody's fault, it was just how things had worked out due to the ship's unexpectedly long dry dock.

One incident I recall where my police background was definitely useful was in preventing a gang fight! A group of school students were crossing the road near to the bridge. One of them made a comment to one of the street boys as he probably knew him from a time when that particular boy had been attending school. The comment, whatever it was, obviously wasn't taken lightly. Quick as a flash, all of the street boys had been summoned from under the bridge, in an attempt to protect the "victim's" reputation, and they were carrying very large rocks. The students, now terrified and no doubt wishing they had remained silent were herded onto the bridge like cattle and cornered by the street boys and the rocks. It all happened in a matter of seconds.

At first, I just stood there wondering what on earth was going on, but then I saw the expressions on the faces of some of the street boys. I realised they were really angry and were seriously intending to throw the rocks at the students. One of the rocks was twice the size of a person's head! I ran into the middle of the scene as there were about twenty metres between the two groups who were facing each other from their battle lines. I shouted at the smallest boy, Reuben, who had the biggest rock, to put it down. I thought that he would obediently obey me as I had a close relationship with him, but he ignored me completely. I then shouted for Matthew the street boy's group leader and he appeared. I yelled at him in something of a panic, "Matthew, you have to stop this! If Reuben throws that rock he will kill one of those kids and go to prison for the rest of his life." I couldn't believe his casual response. "No, he won't. He's a juvenile, nothing will happen." Later I learned that his statement was essentially true.

I was still standing between the two groups so that any rocks would hit me first. I knew that the boys wouldn't throw rocks whilst I was standing there (or so I hoped!) The amazing thing was that there were loads of adults around and no one was doing anything to resolve the problem. They were all just watching and waiting. In the end, Matthew relented and signalled to someone in the other group which called off the whole thing. The students fearfully made their way off the bridge and were chased up the street by the street boys to "see them off." I was amazed at how quickly little cute Reuben had turned into a monster, and how he had blatantly ignored me when I tried to talk to him. It was a lesson in loyalties though and demonstrated to me that their ties to each other as their "street family" were still stronger than their ties to us.

From time to time, the boys were also in trouble with the local police, often for no good reason other than that they were in the wrong place at the wrong time. Several times I felt it necessary to intervene as I knew they hadn't done anything, but most of the time I couldn't be sure. Sometimes, I arrived on the bridge to be told that one or other of the boys was at the police station just up the road, having been detained for theft or some other crime. The law in the Philippines, as mentioned earlier, doesn't allow for juveniles to commit a crime, so they were released after a day or two normally with stories of how they had been beaten up in the police station, which I was unable to verify.

Another day, Malachi, who was nine, was detained and crying outside the mall for allegedly stealing some food. I asked the security guard what he had done and when he told me I felt a bit angry. I knew Malachi was hungry. It sounded like he had tried to relieve someone of their leftover food as they had left the mall, something lots of the boys did, but that this particular person hadn't appreciated it. I asked Malachi if he was hungry and of course, he said "yes" through his tears. So I told him to stop crying and to come with me and I would buy him some food. I told the guard where I was going and off we went. After Malachi had eaten I looked over at the guard and signalled to him that we were leaving the area and he nodded. I told Malachi to be on his way and not to cause any more trouble. Inside, my heart was beating fast and although I was acting and speaking with authority and confidence, I was expecting the guard just to take Malachi back into custody, but he didn't.

Another time Isaac, aged eleven, a boy who I didn't know that well but who seemed to me to be one of the harder boys, got into some trouble in a restaurant. He was alleged to have taken someone's purse. On the few occasions that I had met or seen him, he had been alone and always high on solvents. Once I had seen him repeatedly trying to get a coffee from a machine, only to fall over backwards in the process. He lay on his back on the floor as his eyes rolled back in his head and he shouted nonsense at me. I had never seen anything like that in a child, but I didn't really know what I could do to help him whilst he was in that state. In the end, I had to leave, but the memory stayed with me. On a more sensible occasion, I spoke to him late at night, when he was sitting with the adult men outside a shop near to where he lived. I asked him whether he liked being on the street and he said, "No." He said that there was a problem at home, but wasn't specific.

In relation to the theft allegation, I knew he hadn't done what was alleged. The angry tears and shouting immediately demonstrated to me that here was one unjustly accused. I tried hard not to resent the lady making the accusation, but it was obvious that she had seen the "street boy" and jumped to conclusions because "Well, that's what that type of boy does, isn't it?" I told the security guards that I would vouch for Isaac and led him quietly outside. But the guards were still threatening to call the police and Isaac was distraught. He picked up a rock and motioned to throw it through the window. I stood in the way and reasoned with him.

Fortunately, the DSWD staff suddenly appeared and, as they were feared much more than the police, Isaac made a hasty exit. Joel, who had been watching the scene, didn't run quickly enough and was detained by DSWD, only to be released a few days later. I remember the look on Joel's face pleading with us to do something as I was forced to walk away and leave him with them. We had warned them time and again that if they remained on the street they would eventually be captured and sent to rehab but they didn't listen.

Another desperate situation relates to one of the group leaders, Matthew. I was aware that he had been in and out of rehab over the years and that during one of his stints he had made a commitment to Jesus, through a Christian social worker. Matthew often asked me and other crew members for help saying that he wanted to change his life, especially during conversations online, but when we went to see him and offered to help him he changed the subject or acted as if he didn't know what we were talking about. I knew his background and family situation were traumatic—he had sent me messages online about how much he hated various members of his family. He had been on the street for many years.

On one occasion he wrote a really deep message and posted this to me on Facebook. It's too personal to reprint in full, but it was basically saying that he knew that others were disappointed with his life and that he hated himself because of what he had become and that he was trapped. However, he was inspired to change because of the examples around him and the hope that he could see. I discussed the message with the bridge team and they were surprised, Nick said: "I didn't know they even thought like that." Reading the message, I saw that Matthew was trapped in a big dark hole, but that he was starting to see light at the end of the tunnel.

I contacted a pastor friend and asked if he would be available to see Matthew at the church the day after I had received the message. Then I tried to persuade Matthew to see the pastor with me, but he refused. The pastor finally went to the bridge to meet some of the boys and had a long talk with him. Matthew was really listening as the pastor said that he had to make a definite decision to change his life and that then we would be able to help him. After the pastor left, however, Matthew went back down under the bridge where he flew into a massive temper. He was shouting and swearing and cursing and crying angry tears. He inhaled drugs at top speed, threw things around and moved about in great distress. Nick went to try and help and comfort him, but Matthew shoved him away.

Matthew later said that it was because, while he had been speaking to the pastor, someone had stolen his money from under the bridge. I knew there was more to it than this as it wasn't a lot of money and we offered to replace it which he refused. It was really an extreme reaction and behaviour that we hadn't witnessed before. I wondered if it was a more serious spiritual problem due to things Matthew might have been involved in. Another boy later told us something that confirmed that this was probably the case.

CHAPTER FOURTEEN

The Real Stories

Our bridge team had asked the ship leadership for a Filipino to work on the bridge with us several times. We were still struggling to communicate properly with the boys. We had built friendships and the boys trusted us, but we wanted to have deeper conversations and find ways to really help the boys longer term. Enter Arlene who joined the ship in September 2012, and joined us on the bridge soon after. Her presence was a blessing but also an eye opener as we started to hear the real reasons why the boys were on the street. Although they had given us their real names and some of their basic stories were true, most of the facts about where they were living and other details were lies or exaggerations.

Arlene confirmed what I had suspected for some time, most of the boys lived in Olongapo City and had families and homes to return to. They were on the street for a range of reasons including poverty, broken homes, physical abuse, and rebellion. I believe they lied about where they were from because they thought we would try and take them back to their problem families if we knew they lived locally.

They were used to lying to the police and DSWD about their lives. Sometimes their lies convinced the police not to take action as it would be too much hassle to deal with them if they lived far away. The police told me that they had tried to break up the group under the bridge in the past and had sent the boys back to the various provinces that they claimed to be from, only to have them return to Olongapo a few weeks later. This information also explained the mutterings I had heard that the police didn't have jurisdiction over the boys. It seemed that the authorities had given up trying to break up the group which had become almost impossible to manage as they were like a large family helping and looking out for each other.

It was painful to hear some of the boys' stories as they were similarly traumatic. Simon was embarrassed that his family was poor. His parents were separated and he and his younger sister lived with his Dad who was disabled due to having polio. Simon was collecting plastic from around the city to help his family. This was a common way for people to make a small amount of money, collecting recyclable plastic. They received around five or ten pesos (seven or fourteen pence) for every large bag of plastic. But Simon had grown tired of his work and had dropped out of school when he got involved with the "rugby boys."

Joel's parents were also separated and he believed that his family would never be happy unless they got back together. But, his father had remarried and had three young children with his new wife. Joel told us that he was beaten and made to work long hours at home. Reuben also was beaten by his father who was cruel. (This was confirmed later by a neighbour.)

Adam was one of the boys that worried me the most as he had a learning difficulty making social interaction difficult. He stood next to me and punched me repeatedly in the arm whilst using profanity in English. When I told him to stop, he laughed and moved away but then started doing it again a few seconds later. Now I believe it was drug related, but at the time I wasn't sure why he kept doing it. Adam did have friends in the group but was often alone and was easily influenced to bad behaviour. Unfortunately, some of the other boys took advantage of his disability.

One morning I was walking in the city early at 8:30 am not expecting to see any of the boys as they usually slept until 10 or 11 am. Then I saw Adam. He was walking along the street with his hand up his T-shirt which was over his nose and he was inhaling from a plastic bag. He didn't see me to begin with due to being high on drugs but when I said his name he looked at me. I couldn't believe no one was doing anything as he was in the city centre with lots of people around and it was obvious that he was inhaling solvents. I tried to persuade him to give me the bag so I could buy him some food but he refused and ran off. The image of Adam alone and inhaling solvents early that morning, ingrained itself in my memory. It sounds crazy, but at least when they were in the group they had each other. Conversely, that was also one of the biggest problems: they had been in the group for so long that the group had become their family and the street their home.

Adam said that he had been sent to Olongapo to live with his uncle because his parents didn't want him. He felt that he had just been thrown away like a piece of rubbish. They had kept his sister. Adam just wanted a family of his own. A neighbour or his uncle (we were unable to verify which) gave him a small amount of money every day for food and then let him loose in the city. But all Adam wanted was to be back with his parents and to be loved by them. After he shared his story, Adam sat on the ground in the centre of the bridge. There were people milling all around him heading in both directions, but no one was taking any notice of him. He was invisible. I continued to watch him as he sat there all alone. The expression of pain and anguish on his face was so real that I had to turn my face away. What on earth had happened to Adam to make him hurt this much?

Luke, aged fifteen, was Muslim and often took more drugs than the others because he was grieving over his father's death. He had more respect for us than some of the others, maybe just because he was a little older. I sensed his problems were genuine and that he was deeply unhappy. We repeatedly told the boys that they should go home to their houses and not stay on the street. He told us that his family lived nearby so I asked if we could go and see his house and meet them. He wasn't prepared for this and came up with a lot of excuses, but we applied gentle pressure and eventually, he agreed. His friends thought it was a big joke as he was high on solvents and didn't really think we were serious. They were laughing at him when we said, "Let's go."

We arrived at Luke's house quickly as it was not far from the bridge. It was a surprise as I had believed it would be further away. We were welcomed in, although the family seemed surprised to see us as it was unannounced. I hoped Luke wouldn't get in trouble after we had gone for bringing foreign uninvited guests home, especially Christian ones! Luke's mother was there with about twenty other people including numerous children. They introduced Luke's brother's, who were all married, with their wives and children. They were all living in a tiny space which looked like it consisted of just two rooms with little furniture.

One of the reasons for requesting a visit was to try and get Luke enrolled in school. We needed his birth certificate in order to do this, so we asked his mother for it. She advised that she didn't know where it was and when we checked she didn't even know how old he was or when his birthday was. It was really upsetting as Luke just sat there watching the proceedings with a blank expression on his face as he had obviously heard it all before.

A birth certificate or a certificate of completion of the previous school year was a requirement for annual enrolment at school. Sometimes the paperwork was lost by families or destroyed during typhoons or floods. The result: The child was not allowed to enrol unless they or the parents completed a lengthy process which sometimes involved long distance travel which they couldn't afford. As I subsequently discovered, the whole procedure was very frustrating and time-consuming and didn't always secure the desired outcome. Although school placements were free, many families couldn't afford to pay for their children's lunch and transportation to get there or they needed the children to earn money by working illegally, so they didn't send them to school.

I was appalled that Luke's mother didn't know even basic things about him. She didn't seem to really care and our efforts to obtain his birth certificate came to nothing. I thought to myself, "No wonder he's on the street. I think I would rather be there than in this place." It wasn't just the conditions that were tough, but the lack of care and concern from his mother. If the family had really cared, they could easily have come to the bridge and taken Luke home and away from the drugs. They expressed concern about his solvent abuse to us and after this visit, his older brother did come to the bridge a few times and take him home. However, the concern seemed to fade over time, as if they were just trying to satisfy us in some way.

As we left the place this day, I put my arm around Luke and said, "See, it was okay, us meeting your family, wasn't it?" He smiled and said that it had been fine. He was very cheerful after this, but I couldn't stop thinking about the visit and how naïve I had been in thinking that if he would just go home things would be better.

CHAPTER FIFTEEN

Mark: The Prodigal Son

One day, I turned up at the bridge to find Mark (the boy treated by the dentist before) holding his arm and indicating he was in pain. I asked him what was wrong and he said that he thought it might be broken. Noah, nine years old, also kept spitting out blood that appeared to be coming from one of his teeth. A third boy Simon, twelve, had developed raised lumps all over his hands overnight presumably due to some kind of allergy. I really didn't want to spend another day in the hospital, so I told them that I couldn't take them anywhere immediately as there was no one to stay at the bridge table. Mark began crying as he was in pain, so in the end, I relented and arranged cover at the book table.

At the hospital, I observed that Mark said he was "born again" when asked to specify his faith at the reception. He was very specific about it and made the distinction from being Catholic. I talked to Mark a lot about the Gospel whilst we were waiting and how Jesus was the only answer to the problems in his life, although I didn't know much about his life at this stage. He began crying again whilst Noah was looking on. I asked Noah if he knew why I was trying to help them and he said, "Because you are kind!" I made sure that he knew it was because of Jesus, but I was touched by his comment.

Mark told me that he had spent time in rehab before with a few of our other boys. He told me a lot of really sad things about his life. He said he had been on the street for years and that his ex-girlfriend's family was trying to kill him because they thought he had gotten her pregnant. I was confused because I had seen his profile picture on

Facebook. In what had appeared to be a recent photo he had been in his school uniform, looking clean and of a healthy weight. I challenged him by asking, "Mark, what happened to you? You look good in your Facebook picture, and now you've dropped out of school and are on the street taking drugs?" But the challenge produced further tears, so I just reminded him that Jesus could help him. I felt really sorry for him but couldn't understand what was going on in his life or what I could do practically.

In the end, Noah left the hospital before receiving treatment due to impatience. I got his prescription for him and gave it to his mother. Simon was told he had an allergy and was given a medicinal cream. Mark had an x-ray which revealed that his arm wasn't broken. They gave him a sling for comfort which he seemed to be happy with, probably due to the extra attention it would inevitably bring him. So we left the hospital after only a few hours.

Mark sometimes mentioned a church in the area by name. So I asked him if he wanted us to take him to visit the church and the pastor. He agreed, so off we went one day. We arrived at the church and introduced Mark to the pastor. Mark readily agreed to attend the church at a future date. It all seemed quite easy, and a little too easy in a strange way.

Later, when we discussed the church and the pastor, Mark surprised us all by saying the pastor's name. He then told us that he had already known the pastor that we had introduced him to because it had been his previous church! The revelation was all a bit odd as the pastor hadn't indicated that he knew Mark at all. Mark then told us that in addition to attending the church, he had also been going to a Bible study and had even led Sunday School. We were gradually solving the mystery, or so we thought.

Mark became good friends with Luke, due to their similar ages, but unfortunately most of the time they were high on solvents. I was really concerned about them and their influence on each other. When they were walking along the street, Mark looked miserable and hopeless as he always seemed to. I said, "Mark, you just look so unhappy. What is wrong?" I was shocked when he just began openly crying in the street in front of Luke and passers-by. I looked away as I struggled to contain my own emotion. I could see the deep distress he was in but couldn't help him.

After some time, I asked the other boys about Mark. They said Mark had not been to rehab as he had told us. They said that he had only dropped out of high school a few months earlier and that he had a family at home who loved him. They said his mother was working selling items near the bridge every evening and that we should talk to her. I confronted Mark about his lies and asked him what was really going on. He didn't really tell me and continued to insist that he had been to rehab before. I still had difficulties with the language, and even with translation couldn't seem to get to the bottom of things. Mark knew this and deliberately left things vague. He had been in his final year of high school when he dropped out, so his English was pretty good, but he kept it quiet. I could tell that he understood a lot of what we, as crew members, were saying to each other and he used this for his own purposes at times.

I kept trying to persuade Mark to go back to school and re-enrol for the year. As it was September, he had only missed a few months. I knew his teachers would give him a chance if he asked them. He kept agreeing and then changing his mind at the last minute. I got really frustrated with him, but eventually, he agreed to re-enrol the following Monday.

Luke also told us that his family was thinking of moving to Manila so that he would be able to go to school. He said they might be leaving at any time. We had promised all of the boys that they could visit the ship before we left, so we took Mark and Luke for an initial visit. The other boys weren't happy, but we justified it on the basis that the two of them would be going to school soon and may not have another chance to visit the ship. They got really upset, accusing me of favouritism. Finally, they sent Joel as a representative to question me. He boldly confronted me but when I explained the situation carefully to him he accepted the explanation and pulled the other boys away. It was hard to leave them all behind at the gate, but we didn't have the capacity to take them all on the ship at this stage, especially when they had been inhaling solvents.

When we arrived on the ship, all of the crew were really friendly as they had heard a lot about the boys. I introduced them to some of the crew members who already knew their names as they had seen pictures of them. They were walking around as if they were royalty. Luke went up to everyone he saw and loudly said "Hi!" and waved. It was pretty funny. When we went into the book-fair we discovered that the boys were fascinated by the books. They both sat on the floor in the hobbies section, pulled books off the shelves about all sorts of subjects, and just sat there looking at the pictures. It occurred to me that maybe they didn't have the chance to look at books normally, and it made me sad. In England, we take having access to good books and reading material for granted.

After they had finished with the books, we took them for a tour of the ship. They especially enjoyed having photos taken wearing the captain's hat on the bridge (control centre) of the ship. They drank juice in the dining room and then it was time to leave. Mark indicated that he was cold so one of the crew gave him her jumper. Of course, Luke also wanted one so I gave him one of mine but he complained loudly because it didn't have a hood! Later, all of the clothing was either sold or swapped amongst the boys anyway. The only boy who didn't sell things was Matthew (the leader) and he accumulated a large number of our items. We took the two boys back to the bridge area after their visit and then went back to the ship.

Over time, I became close to Mark as I wanted to get to the root of his troubles and try to help him. I especially wanted to see him back in school. He told us one day that he didn't want to stay on the street with the others that evening. He was worried about their influence as he was trying to stay clear of the solvents. So, we took him with us to the ship again. That decision caused a massive outburst amongst the other boys who suddenly appeared in a group as we were leaving and started running around us shouting. They even broke through the barrier past the security guards and tried to follow us but they were stopped. I was forced to tell them that we were only taking Mark with us.

When they protested, I told them it was because they had been inhaling solvents and I could smell it on them. We started a practice of getting them to breathe so that we could smell if they were high or not. The other boys were really angry, apart from a boy called Paul who didn't even bother to breathe to try and prove that he wasn't high. He knew that he was and that our decision was fair. Fairness was very important to the boys and we were careful to try not to show partiality. It was difficult when the boys lied, we didn't always get it right. Mark pulled a face at the others as we walked off, which I wasn't happy about as he was deliberately taunting them. Later, we learned that Mark too was taking drugs every day and that he was deceiving us, but street boys don't generally tell tales about each other so we weren't aware of this at the time.

During Mark's second visit to the ship, he wanted to play a game of chess. Mark managed to beat me which I was surprised about. I'm not great at chess, but I know how to play and didn't expect to be beaten by a street kid who was damaging his brain by inhaling solvents every day! Mark then mentioned that he had been a chess champion at his school. I told him again that he must make sure he went back to school during the week and that I would be accompanying him to see his tutor. He also agreed to go back to his house and live with his family.

After the ship visit, we took Mark back to the city and went to meet his mum who was selling food in the evenings. His mum was really nice and didn't understand why Mark was on the street. She said he had his own room at home and enough food to eat. She mentioned that initially there had been a problem with a girlfriend that had started the issue. Mark said that he would go home with his mum and stay there. Again, it all seemed a bit too easy.

However, we soon found that we were going around in circles with Mark. The following day, when we came to set up the book table on the bridge, he was sleeping there alone. Usually, there were various boys sleeping on the bridge in a huddle waiting for us to arrive in the morning. We woke them up when we arrived for ministry. But this time Mark was there alone. I woke him up and asked him why he was there and what had happened. His clothes were really very dirty in comparison to the other boys, who somehow kept themselves relatively clean. Mark said there were problems at his house. When we pushed him for more information, he said that his older brother often beat him up when drunk. I went with Mark later that day to talk to his mum and brother about the problems and to try to resolve them so he could go home. His mum said that actually there was no problem and his brother told us that they just wanted Mark back at home.

We repeated this scenario every day with Mark, arriving to find him asleep on the bridge after having promised us that he would go home the day before. Many times I sat on the floor with him on arrival and talked to him about his life. At times he covered his ears and said, "No English, no English," pretending not to understand, but I knew he just didn't want to hear what I had to say. It was at this time that a local woman walked past and pulling a face said to me, "They're rugby boys, don't you know?" as if it was a secret. She seemed to expect me to say, "Oh my goodness, yes you're right. I must get away from them at once. Thank you so much for telling me" Instead, I said simply, "I love them and Jesus does too." Her comment summed up local attitudes even amongst some of the Christians. It was as if the "rugby boys" were some sort of alien species that had invaded. I heard many similar comments, but this one stuck in my mind as a good representation.

I couldn't find evidence that Mark was taking drugs, but the other boys were so upset with him that they broke their golden rule about telling tales to tell us that he was. I knew that there had been something going on because there was a big division in the group. Mark was on one side and all of the other boys on the other and they were leaving him to sleep alone. I thought it was because the other boys were inhaling solvents and he wasn't, but I wasn't sure if he was deceiving us as he had lied before. I really couldn't understand what was going on and got more and more frustrated with Mark.

The day before we were due to go to Mark's school, I made him promise again that he would go home, have a shower, and change into clean clothes so that he looked presentable at his school. When we arrived at the bridge, in the morning, he was there again asleep, but at least he had changed his clothes and looked somewhat cleaner. We went to his school and a teacher lectured us for an hour about the pitfalls of dropping out of school and missing classes before we convinced him to allow Mark to re-enrol. The teacher said we needed to speak to Mark's specific tutor for her to arrange a special test for him to catch up. Mark's tutor said that he was a good student and confirmed that he had been chess champion at the school the previous year and had won a lot of money for the school in a tournament in Manila. She said to Mark, "What's happened to you? You used to be handsome!" She was talking about his massive weight-loss and general state of unhealthiness due to drug addiction. She was kind and agreed to the special test to re-enrol him. The date for the test was arranged.

Shortly after that, I was walking in the city in the evening with Arlene. As we approached the bridge leading back to the ship, I saw a lone figure standing in the shadows watching the people walking past. He was unsteady on his feet and rocking backwards and forwards holding a plastic bag in his hand. As I moved nearer, I saw it was Mark. He ran away when he saw me and tried to hide but didn't get very far and so he sat on the ground, behind a large pillar, in the shadows, breathing heavily. I sat beside him on the ground, which was dirty and really stank, and when I put my arm around his shoulders I smelt the intoxicatingly strong smell of the solvent.

The boys had stopped taking Rugby and had moved on to a door sealant called Vulcaseal which was stronger. It was all over Mark and he reeked of it. I covered my nose. I remember this was the only time where the thought ran through my mind that I could see how addiction to the smell was created because it was really intoxicating. I knew I needed to be careful not to breathe much of it in, but Mark was really very high. He was vacant and staring ahead, and then he began crying again as I tried to talk to him. I asked him why he was determined to destroy himself and what was it that had made him so unhappy, but he didn't answer.

Arlene went to get Mark's mum who was working nearby because I didn't know what to do and I didn't want to leave him alone and miserable. His mum got very upset and begged him to come home. Mark got up when she arrived and stumbled away as we all watched him go. I followed and tried to talk to him again, sharing a bit of my life before I became a Christian and how miserable I had been. His hopelessness reminded me of my old life when I was immersed in drink, gambling and meaningless relationships. I knew Mark was listening as I shared the hope that I had found with him, but he didn't respond. Eventually, we had to leave him, alone and staring vacantly ahead of himself hanging over a railing. I was really worried that he wouldn't make it through the night if he inhaled any more solvents, but he didn't seem to care and our attention and concern was only making things worse.

After that night, we experienced serious problems with Mark at the bridge. Sometimes I wasn't even aware that he was there, but then I would catch a glimpse of him standing at a distance staring at us. I knew he had been abusing solvents, even though he always denied it, so I walked over to him but he ran away. I chased after him and he shouted, "No, Ma'am Natalie, no." as he tried to hide under some cardboard, because he didn't want me to smell the drugs on him. The smell was very strong and I told him that he wouldn't be able to go back to school if he couldn't sort out his addiction. But he was playing games with us, encouraging the other boys to take solvents with no intention of stopping himself. Unbelievably, his behaviour was about to get even worse.

CHAPTER SIXTEEN

Paul: A Special Friendship

One special story is that of Paul, aged fourteen. Paul wasn't around that much at the beginning of our ministry. He was taller than the other boys and seemed tougher in many ways. He had obviously been on the street for a long time and was missing all of his front teeth. In a small way, to look at him reminded me of my brother James who died in a car accident in 2002. But that was where the similarity ended. Paul was rude and obnoxious. He made it clear that he didn't appreciate us being there and didn't like us. He didn't like the influence we were having on the younger boys. He took what he could get from us and left. He was obviously using us.

Despite his behaviour, we tried to treat all the boys as equals, so as not to create problems with allegations of favouritism. Several times, when Paul arrived, I tried to talk to him but he rudely ignored me or began talking to one of the other boys as if he hadn't heard me. He deliberately annoyed me by sitting in the way or just generally being a nuisance. He rarely smiled and would hold his hand out to make demands and say, "Give me!" all of the time. On one occasion, he became irritated and angry with one of the younger boys and kicked him hard in the ribs. I was shocked as I hadn't seen such violence directed from one boy to another within the group.

However, I saw at other times, that Paul was generous with the others and shared his food with the younger boys even though he didn't have much himself. I realised that he had become accustomed to fighting for survival after many years on the street. Although Paul was a tall boy he was very thin and underweight. He came to our table but then just lazed around sleeping underneath it or on a chair nearby. I noticed that he started to come more frequently but he still didn't really address us or pay any attention to us. Sometimes he took the guitar and started singing out of tune in a language nobody really understood which he described as "street language." I was joking around with some boys, one day, and placed one of their arms around Paul. He got really mad and loudly said, "No!" He grabbed my arm, and demonstrated what I had done, and made it clear he didn't like it. I got the message. He also told one of the other boys off when they were cuddling me saying, "You are fifteen years old, not a baby."

Over time, I began to like Paul. Some of the ladies selling things regularly on the bridge asked him to man their stalls whilst they went to get drinks. He seemed to be trustworthy and never tried to take anything. Once I saw Reuben, one of the younger boys, approaching an old beggar man who was sound asleep on the bridge. He picked up his begging pot, tipped the money out into his hand, put the empty pot back, and sauntered off casually grinning as he walked past us. Paul looked at me as I tried to process what I had just witnessed, he saw that I was open-mouthed at Reuben's audacity and didn't know what to do about the blatant thieving. Paul grinned but confronted Reuben by standing in front of him and without needing to say anything, held his hand out for the money. Reuben automatically gave it to him due to the age hierarchy of authority amongst the boys. Paul then woke the man up gently by tapping him and gave the money back. Paul began appearing at the bridge, every day, with or without the other boys. He didn't say hello but held up his hand for a high-five, then he sat down and hung around for most of the day.

A local pastor that came to the bridge said that he knew Paul and that he had been following him around the city for at least a year trying to give him food. When the pastor first arrived, Paul was lying on the ground and he acknowledged the pastor. The pastor ordered him to sit up in order to show respect, and he obeyed, grinning to himself. I noted that he did have some respect for authority. Paul confirmed through the pastor that he really didn't like us when we had first arrived on the bridge. When we asked for a reason he said that he didn't know why. The pastor told us later that Paul was one of the worst street boys and the most difficult to handle, a fact we were already becoming aware of.

Over time, the barriers came down and I saw that Paul was warming to us, although he would never have admitted it. One day, we were having a conversation whilst he was lying in his favourite position, on the ground underneath the table. During the conversation, he pointed his fingers at me mimicking a gun signal. I laughed at him and said, "Why, do you want to kill me?" I thought he would say "Yes" or "I already have" or something, but he said "No" very definitely and watched to see my reaction. So I asked him "Why?" and he said, "Because you are good." I was caught off guard by the assertion from a boy like Paul with real attitude. It struck me that he wasn't messing around and that he had taken some time to reach his conclusion. I gathered my thoughts and said: "Only because of Jesus." And he nodded to acknowledge this. We had this same conversation several times after that and it became a bit of a joke, but I will always remember that first time being caught off guard and realising that we were having an impact on the boys, albeit slowly.

Paul often asked to borrow my MP3 player and listened to the music or watched the music videos for hours. The boys always found the video of me and some others from the ship singing *Kay Buti Buti Mo Panginoon* (The Lord is good) on the MP3 player and played it loudly singing along. The younger boys also borrowed my camera sometimes and took hundreds of pictures of themselves posing. I tried to keep an eye on the location of these items when they were using them. But, there was a time when I wasn't paying enough attention and Paul wandered off with my MP3 player. I waited for a while, convinced he would come back, but then started to worry, not really about the item but about what I would do if he didn't return.

Local people saw that I was looking around and they had seen Paul leave. One man said, "That's the last you'll see of that. You'd better go to the police." And other people expressed similar concerns. But I said with more confidence than I felt, "He will come back." After ten or fifteen minutes, Paul sauntered back casually carrying the MP3 player and some rice that he was eating, as if nothing was wrong. I was relieved and just said to him, "Please stay here if you have that" and he nodded. I could see from his nonchalant expression that he was testing me to see if I trusted him or trying to prove that he was trustworthy.

Really Paul was testing us constantly to see if we practised what we were preaching. I liked him as his loyalty was harder to gain and therefore worth more. Some of the other boys were quite superficial in their loyalties, as evidenced by the thefts and other problems. But once we had gained Paul's trust, we didn't lose it. His background was quite confusing, but we established that he had been on and off the street since he was seven and had spent a year in rehab at twelve. To start with, he wasn't really interested in changing his life and spoke about wanting to "still go around" the city. Over time, this changed and I believed that he might really be serious about wanting to leave the street.

Then one of the older boys told me that Paul was very ill and had been vomiting blood. He said there had been an X-Ray which showed a hole in Paul's lung and that it was really serious. I was very upset as I was close to him by this point. Later that day, I was coming out of the mall, with my "halo-halo," (a mixture of all types of food including beans, sweetcorn, jelly, milk and ice-cream and a dessert delicacy in the Philippines!) which I bought for lunch every day, and I saw Paul standing at the entrance to the mall. He was leaning inside the door but he knew that he wasn't allowed to go in as the security guards would stop him. He wasn't focusing on me as I was coming towards him because he was obviously high on solvents, but as I got nearer he saw and acknowledged me. He then put my arm around his neck, a practice the older boys adopted as a more manly sign of affection than the younger one's cuddles.

We walked together back towards the bridge and I decided to broach the subject of his illness with him. I had already determined to make him go to the hospital but knew I had to handle it carefully, he might refuse if I put pressure on him. I said, "I hear that you are ill and have been coughing blood." He just nodded. I told him that it made me sad as I didn't want something bad to happen to him. I asked him if he would go to the hospital with me. He didn't want to, but when we got back to the bridge he pointed at my "halo-halo" and asked me to give it to him. It was my lunch every day and I never gave it away, the boys accepted this and didn't ask me for it. In fact, if a new boy who didn't know the rules came by and asked me for my "halo-halo" the other boys told them off advising them that it was my lunch.

On this day, I was so upset about Paul's illness that I gave it to him. His eyes brightened and he seemed surprised as he hadn't really expected me to give it to him. He then got the spoon and started feeding all of the other younger boys with bits from it before having any himself. It was quite a sight as they all sat on the floor waiting to be fed with a spoon, even though they were eleven and twelve years old. I then asked him again about the hospital and later, with the help of his friends, persuaded him to go. He agreed, but only if Mark accompanied him.

At the hospital, I decided it was time that he really understood the Gospel. I really wasn't sure if he had been listening before and I wasn't sure how ill he really was. Arlene translated the discussion. The first things we established were that he thought it would make him a better person if he went to church. He said it with such sincerity and I could see that he really thought he was a terrible person in the sight of God. He then said that he couldn't go into a church building because he didn't know how to pray and that he couldn't pray because he was too dirty. Later, I thought a lot about Paul's sincere (but wrong) beliefs about God and I wondered how many others felt like this. In the West, we are arrogantly ignoring God and acting as if He doesn't exist. But then here was Paul who didn't dare to approach God, thinking he would be rejected. I explained the truth to Paul, and when I told him how Jesus died on the cross for his sin, he immediately said that he knew this already because I had taught it to them on the bridge. Hearing this was a huge encouragement as I hadn't been sure how much had been understood.

When we went in to see the doctor, Paul and Mark both had tests and x-rays. They weren't very well behaved and kept messing around with equipment, leaving and going outside and wandering around. When the nurse couldn't find Paul's pulse the two boys thought it was hilarious and Paul grabbed his heart and acted as if he was about to keel over and die on the spot. I was unhappy with the doctor's attitude. She looked at the boys with distaste throughout the proceedings and spoke about them as if they weren't there when giving their results.

Mark's x-ray was completely clear, again evidencing his lack of long-term drug abuse. Paul's x-ray showed deep scar tissue on his lung and the doctor told us he had tuberculosis (TB.) I asked her if it was advanced and she said yes. She didn't show any compassion or any love towards him at all. I was left to ask the questions about what would happen and, not really knowing anything about the disease, I was really concerned. She gave us a prescription for Paul and we left. Paul and Mark were joking around, but I knew it had to be false bravado on Paul's part as it was serious. I was annoyed with Mark for trivialising things, but realised that his immaturity meant that he didn't know any better.

It also hit me that TB is very contagious and that Paul often shared his food with the other boys. He even ate from the same spoon. I too had not really taken extra precautions with the boys, but I was less worried about this as I had been vaccinated. I was always careful not to eat from or drink from the same things as the boys, which is the main way the disease is spread. I told Paul that he mustn't share his food anymore, but it took a while for him to remember this as it had always been his practice. To start with I reminded him, but on occasionally, I also forgot and one day I even encouraged him to share with another boy. He looked surprised and I thought he was being less than generous until he gave the water to the other boy and then said to me, "But I'm sick." I tried to stop the other boy from drinking it, but it was too late. As far as I'm aware, none of the others caught TB from Paul.

In any event, after leaving the hospital we went to a pharmacy to buy Paul's medicine. I looked him in the eyes and told him that whilst taking the medicine he mustn't take any drugs or it could kill him due to the interaction. He promised me, but added, "But I will be hungry."

I responded, "Right, if that's the reason I promise you that I will make sure you have enough food every day until the ship leaves."

To prove that I meant what I had said, we took Paul and Mark to a restaurant and said they could order what they wanted. They both ate a lot and asked for more rice. After eating, Arlene and Mark were outside waiting and I was left with Paul who was finishing his rice. He looked at me and said seriously, "Ma'am Natalie, thank you for trying to help us." I nodded but had to look away because the tears came again. Paul was a hardened street boy saying thank you, maybe for the first time in years. He finished his rice and put his thumb up to indicate that he had enjoyed it. When we got outside they both said they were full so we went back to the ship, leaving them to go and find somewhere to sleep.

CHAPTER SEVENTEEN

Loss of Control

The next day Paul was very quiet and there was a problem between him and Mark. I knew immediately what it was, so I asked Paul, "Did Mark try and get you to take drugs with him last night, and now he is mad because you refused?" He didn't say anything at first, but I persisted and eventually, he nodded. There was an ongoing conflict for Paul after that as he tried to keep his loyalties to his friends and also to us at the same time.

My promise to ensure Paul had proper food every day brought its own issues. Some might describe the promise as unwise or rash. I knew that if necessary I could arrange for funds to be transferred from my personal account in England so it wasn't an empty promise. The problem really was how best to fulfil it. The issue of what to do when someone asked me for food was (and still is) a constant battle because I found myself thinking, "Who am I to decide whether this person eats or not today?" Knowing that I had the financial capability to buy food for them most of the time meant that I often relented, unless I could see that it would do more harm than good, for example, professional beggars. But I had to balance that with the knowledge that I couldn't feed everyone. Mostly I just settled for buying food for people that specifically asked for it or offering food instead of money to those asking for the latter.

We realised straight away that we needed to begin some kind of feeding programme, but didn't really know where to start or who to ask. We asked the ship leadership but they said they didn't have the budget for it, and we had already been advised earlier in the ministry that we mustn't allow the ministry with the boys to turn into anything long term. I knew when I made the promise to Paul that we couldn't just feed him. We would need to feed all of our regular boys. We borrowed and begged money from crew members on the ship who gave generously to help us. Most crew members knew of our work on the bridge as they saw us when visiting the city and I had asked for prayer several times at the weekly prayer meeting. Also, every time any of the four hundred crew members went into the city the boys asked them, "Where is Ma'am Natalie?" and told them that I was their friend.

So, to begin with, whilst we were trying to establish something more official through local churches, we took the boys twice a day to various street food stands and bought them all food. Unfortunately, this caused fights every day as the boys argued about who could have which item and complained that one of them had more than another. Also, other boys that we didn't know would try and join the group in order to get food and inevitably there were tears when things went wrong.

On one really bad day, Paul had been asking me all day if we could take them to a particular place to eat as there were only four of them. I said it would be okay if no further boys appeared, but by the end of the day, there were more than seven boys. I told him we were just going to our normal stand as it was cheaper. Paul got really upset and angry. Then he sat on the ground and refused to eat. Some of the other boys also joined him and refused even to look at me or talk to me. Mark took the lead in the rebellion as usual. Suddenly he turned to me and said in a voice thick with hatred, "Me, no back to school, no back to school."

This was one of the only occasions when I totally lost my temper with them. Mark's comments, after all the effort I had made in getting him re-enrolled, really made me angry. I knew he had been waiting for this chance to rebel as he wasn't really interested in going back to school and that he wouldn't change his mind having made the statement. I shouted at them that they were ungrateful and I told Mark that I didn't care whether he went back to school or not. As far as I was concerned if he threw away his life it was his business and I really didn't care anymore as I'd had enough. I was really upset, so we left. Arlene went back after a few minutes to buy the food for Paul that he had requested. I felt guilty as I knew he was dealing with his illness and it was Mark that had really made me angry.

The next day, when we arrived at the bridge, the boys were all sleeping there as usual, so I went straight over to Paul and apologised if I had upset him the day before. He accepted it immediately and although things were a bit strained at first, as it was the first time the boys had seen me lose my temper and they were shocked, they returned to normal after a while. I realised that Paul had believed that I had broken my promise about the food and, as was often the case, the language barrier had caused the confusion.

CHAPTER EIGHTEEN

Local Churches: Please Help Us!

At this time, we approached several churches in the area to ask for help with a basic feeding programme. The idea was that it would just be a temporary programme for up to ten boys and that, as most of the boys had made decisions that they wanted to leave the street, the programme would only continue until we had found them new places to live.

Unfortunately, the local churches didn't really understand our situation. They were all keen to help when we said we were from Logos Hope, but as soon as we mentioned who we were working with and what we needed help with, they backed away. Again it was as if being a "rugby boy" made them somehow less human. We received responses including, "Our members don't really know how to deal with that kind of boy" and, "Here are a few hundred pesos" and, "We will need all sorts of paperwork, a detailed plan of your goals and objectives" etc. One church, that did have a heart for the ministry, was already involved in so many other ministries, that they were unable to really get involved in helping us, although they did try. It was pretty frustrating but we realised we would have to go it alone for the time being. Local people often approached us on the bridge to tell us how kind we were and to thank us for caring for their street children, but most were unwilling to be involved themselves.

I realised that even Christians didn't know how to help the boys, had other priorities, or were unwilling. In many cases, I think people wanted to help but were afraid that their help wouldn't be appreciated or that they might get attacked or rejected in some way. In most cases, the boys had become invisible to people as they were so used to seeing them under the bridge inhaling solvents, they had become desensitised and considered it normal. They didn't think about the long-term damage the solvents were doing and that the boys were just children.

A new believer friend, when speaking about evangelism, said to me, "If you see someone standing in front of a car about to get run over, you pull them out of the way, right?" His faith was so new and the Gospel had hit home so powerfully, without any of the confusion that blinds us over time, that he could see the reality for all people. It was the same with the "rugby boys"; they were killing themselves gradually day by day and often Christians were just ignoring them for a number of different reasons.

One local church was very helpful to us in many ways, they allowed us to store our equipment from the bridge in their building on a daily basis. We were really grateful, and sometimes the members spoke about joining us at the bridge, but nobody came for more than a few minutes at a time in the end. I mention the next incidents, not as a criticism of the individual church but because I believe this is a representation of how many local churches and church members would behave. I hope readers will use the experiences to educate and inform Christians and churches so that they can adapt not just to tolerate the children, but to really love and care for them as well. I really hope not to offend or upset any individuals by detailing the next few incidents, but I think it is necessary to highlight the type of behaviour that can alienate, reject or upset a street child who has already experienced these things in abundance.

The sad thing was that the boys accompanied us into the church every day, as they helped us carry boxes and tables and other things. The members didn't take the opportunities to engage with them. The boys occasionally took a shower in the restroom area of the church, not by invitation but by locking themselves in the bathroom and stripping off before we realised what was going on. I was worried about the water everywhere afterwards. The church leaders were okay about the mess. But at other times, people withdrew and ignored them when the boys went into the church. I was desperate to get the boys introduced into a church and was so disappointed by the missed opportunity.

One day, Mark and Reuben went in with us and members of the church youth were doing a craft activity together in a group at tables. Mark stood at a distance and stared at the activity. I could tell he would have loved to have joined in, but there was an invisible wall, a barrier that I could see and I'm sure Mark could too. It was like he was looking into a house from outside and wasn't allowed in. Just watching him made my eyes fill with tears for the hundred millionth time as I said, "Come on, let's go." Then I put my arm around his shoulders and led him away.

Another time, Reuben picked up a leaflet advertising a youth event, but a church member quickly took it away from him whilst muttering something. I could tell that they wouldn't be welcome to attend. The church members and leadership were very polite and helpful to us as foreigners and members of the Logos Hope, but what about their own Filipino children right on their doorstep? Someone needed to take responsibility and help the boys. Why not the church? What would Jesus do?

CHAPTER NINETEEN

Feeding Programme

We gave up approaching churches after a while, and happened to meet a ship volunteer, Zee on the way back to the ship one evening. (Crew members served on the ship for one or two years at a time and travelled to the ship from countries all around the world. Generally, the ship volunteers were local people that joined the ship in a particular port and remained on-board for the duration of the port, maybe for three or four weeks.) Arlene and I were discussing our desire for a temporary feeding ministry to try and give the boys the chance to come off the solvents. We told Zee how desperate we were for someone to help us as we had been working with the boys for a long time and had built strong relationships with them.

Zee offered us an immediate solution which sounded too good to be true. Her family was renting business premises in the city with a large room on the ground floor that was suitable for providing food for the boys every day. Its primary purpose was as a shop but the family lived in the rooms upstairs. There was also a pool table in the room, which could be used with supervision. It was the kind of offer we had been desperately waiting and praying for. We worked out a plan to provide two meals a day on a temporary basis. We obtained donations from our ship friends to pay for the food. We were just so grateful for the suggestion and the willingness that accompanied it. The book-fair manager's face was a picture when I mentioned this to him, as he was already very worried that the ministry was becoming too large for us to handle. But, he allowed us to go ahead on the basis that we were funding the project ourselves and that it would be temporary. Little did we know that we were about to open a huge can of worms!

Zee also told us about a Christian couple who had been volunteering on the ship who had previously taken in boys from problem families. She told us that they considered that fostering the children was their ministry and that they might be willing to consider taking in some of our boys. We didn't realise that the couple hadn't taken street boys before. We asked her to put us in touch with them as soon as possible. I was having trouble sleeping, as each boy and what to do with him was going around and around in my head all of the time, especially as the ship's time in Subic Bay had to be drawing to a close, or so I thought. We had a core group of only nine or ten boys left, as many of the older boys were working and some of the younger ones had gone home or back to school.

We went to visit the premises for the proposed feeding programme and couldn't quite believe it. It was enormous with a large long table in the centre and the promised pool table in a separate area. It was really perfect for our purposes. We were introduced to Zee's family who were willing to fit the cooking and supervision of the feeding ministry around their business activities. I don't think any of us really knew what we were letting ourselves in for, but we were all willing to give it a shot.

We started straight away by inviting the boys to come and have lunch with us from the bridge. They were intrigued and followed us in a line through the city, not knowing what to expect. It took twenty minutes to locate them all and get them ready. They seemed a bit dazed and confused at first, but they followed us nevertheless. On arrival, the excited chatter diminished as we walked up the steps outside and rang the doorbell. We walked inside and into the big hall and there was the table already laid with dishes and utensils. There was utter and complete silence as the boys walked in and looked around. They really didn't know what to make of it all and were totally overwhelmed. They just stood near to the table not knowing what to do, until the father of the family told them to go and wash their hands in the bathroom and prepare to eat. Without a word, they proceeded single file to the bathroom to do as they were told. The silence continued for another ten minutes or so as the food was dished up and we prayed and began to eat. They were in complete shock and were very polite and well behaved. Gradually, the normal chatter returned, which was a relief as it was strange to see them so quiet and subdued.

After eating, they were allowed to stay for a little while and use the pool table. They were also allowed to take a shower in the bathroom area. Then we said we would collect them later as they were to come back at 6 pm for another meal. I noted that Paul was the only one who appeared not to have taken solvents that day. We had started the feeding programme because of his medical diagnosis, but really it was something we had wanted to do for a while.

Later, our team discussed the first day. The boys had all returned at 6 pm as planned and everything went smoothly. They were very polite throughout the day and expressed their thanks to the family and to us. The family began developing a relationship with the boys straight away which was great to see and something that I hadn't anticipated would happen when we set the ministry in motion.

During one of the sessions, I became aware that my eating habits were a fascination to the boys. They watched me eat with concern and asked frequently why I was eating the chicken before the rice. I explained that, if a person is not used to eating rice, their body needs to adjust to it gradually, but they couldn't understand this and saw it as most irregular and strange. Reuben watched me carefully and one day jumped up from his seat at the table before rushing around to my seat. He grabbed my spoon and fork from me, swapped them around, and exclaimed, "No no no, Ma'am Natalie," I swapped back when he wasn't looking, but it was no good because he always noticed and repeated the whole thing again. This left me, and everyone else, in fits of laughter, as it brought back memories of primary school and being shouted at for eating with my knife and fork the wrong way around.

The team discussed how we were going to take the ministry forward. The boys said they inhaled solvents because they were hungry. We knew that it was part of the reason, but we suspected there was a lot more to it than that. We decided to put their assertion to the test. It wasn't a game or an experiment with the children. Our ultimate goal was to see if the boys could come off the solvents by providing them with enough food, thus encouraging them to think about their lives and futures. We were also conscious that it was unfair to boys like Paul, who were making a real attempt to come off the drugs if we forced them into an environment where they were mixing with others who had taken drugs. The smell that emanated from the culprits was after all extremely intoxicating.

So, we told the boys in advance that they would only be allowed into the building for their lunch and dinner if they hadn't taken any solvents during the day. We tested their truthfulness by smelling them, a practice we had already adopted on previous occasions. Some of the boys tried to get around the rules by making an exhaling sound without breathing any air out, but generally, we could tell. Unfortunately, the restriction turned our peaceful gatherings into a war.

CHAPTER TWENTY

Teething Problems

On the first day, only two boys, Paul and Adam, were allowed in and we turned the others away at the door. Paul had been solvent free for a while and was counting the days. He was becoming more energetic as he came off the solvents and more willing to stand against the others. Adam had been somewhere else for the day so he hadn't spent time with the others and therefore hadn't taken any drugs. We saw the massive influence the group mentality and peer pressure was having on them all. The excluded boys didn't accept their fate. At first, they stood silently outside, but then the insults began. They shouted personal things at me, accusing me of favouritism. They cursed and swore until they were told off by Zee's father, who was not impressed. The worst thing was that the gate at the entrance to the premises was made of metal bars with gaps, so they watched us eating from the doorway for the whole meal, which made us and the other boys feel really bad. But we knew we had to stick to our rules.

After the first few days, the boys knew that we meant what we said, and most of the time they didn't show up if they had taken solvents. Mark was the only one who sometimes made the deliberate decision to take drugs rather than eat and he was still having a negative influence on the others. When he did attend, it was noted that his clothes were so dirty that they left a mark on his chair. I still didn't know what had happened to him to make him so indifferent to his life. We had a few problems with Reuben also refusing to do as he was told and to stop playing pool when he was meant to, but things were generally peaceful.

There were several days when I caught the boys red-handed, inhaling solvents in the daytime before we were due for the evening meal. Once, in the market area, I walked up behind them and could tell they were high. They denied it, but then I smelt them and confirmed it, so I told them not to bother coming to the meal. Reuben was one of the boys I was closest to at that time and I was especially sad to see him abusing solvents, but unfortunately, he didn't seem to have the will to take a stand and was often excluded from our meals. Whenever we excluded them, the boys got really angry and upset, as if we hadn't given them fair warning.

One day I was travelling in a jeepney when I saw a group of them in the street on the opposite side of the road to the feeding ministry venue blatantly inhaling solvents. I couldn't believe that they would do it right outside the feeding premises, so I jumped out of the jeepney and confronted them. They looked really guilty and tried to hide the evidence, but it was too late. I excluded them from the evening meal. Luke gave me the remainder of his drugs in the plastic bag and told me to throw it on the roof. They walked down the road with me trying to persuade me to change my mind. I hated to exclude them but I had to be firm for the sake of the other boys, so I refused. They followed me, calling me names and using bad words, which really upset me.

Our principle was to start again every day and give them another chance, no matter what they had done the day before. So, they said sorry and we said it was okay and tried to forget that any really bad things had happened. The boys were so horrible at times that they were apologising every day, and sometimes for really bad and hurtful behaviour. They started saying, "Really, it's okay?" and, "Why do you always forgive us?" This was obviously a great opportunity to tell them that we forgave them for their sin against us because Jesus had forgiven us for our sins against Him. It was much more effective than just telling them that this was how Christians should behave. They could really see it and see that we loved them despite the way they treated us at times.

I made a big mistake one day due to not being flexible enough. In my mind, we were trying to help a specific group of nine or ten boys.

This is the number that we were paying to feed and the number that we had been working with for some time. They were the boys that we knew well and wanted to see leaving the street for better lives.

The problem was that sometimes there would be an extra boy or two appearing, having slept with the others overnight for a number of reasons, usually relating to problems at home. The dilemma for me was what to do with the extra boys. I envisioned a nightmare scenario where, instead of the feeding ministry becoming smaller and therefore less expensive as we re-housed the boys, it just got larger and larger as we picked up the boys on the fringes. I knew that many of the other boys didn't have enough to eat at home and we didn't want to advertise our feeding programme widely, as we just didn't have the funding to continue it long term. We were relying on donations from crew members with no other funding. The food was costing around twelve hundred pesos (seventeen pounds) a day. It was meant to be a temporary solution, providing somewhere for the boys to come off solvents and to go from there to a new home environment.

We did see massive changes in the boys after only a few days, as they came out of their drug-induced haze and started thinking about their lives and their futures. They came back to life and there were a lot more smiles and energy.

The worst thing about the situation was that we would have loved to have taken all of the extra boys in and helped them as well, but we just didn't have the capacity, so we had to say no. On one particular day, an additional boy, Jonah, was with the other boys and he obviously wanted to eat with us. We said it wasn't possible but the other boys protested, telling us that his dad had been recently murdered or had murdered someone, I can't remember which, as we often heard stories like this. The other boys said that they would share their food with him. I should've agreed to the suggestion as it was fairly reasonable, but I felt I had to stick to my guns to stop them inviting all of their friends. This caused a big problem for some of the boys who thought I was being cruel to exclude one boy.

We went and ate, but the atmosphere was sad as Jonah was sitting outside. His friend inside, Joel, developed an attitude and was determined that he would get his way. I automatically reacted against this as he tried to get around me when I had already said no. He said he was going to give his food to Jonah outside. I told him not to, but he was really insistent, and eventually, I lost my temper with him. I shouted at him that it was our money and that we were paying for them as individuals to eat, that they should be grateful and not start placing conditions or making demands of us, and that we decided who to invite.

Joel stood up and shouted, "Why didn't you tell us that you were paying for this?" I left the table and went outside, as I was really upset and frustrated. Jonah was sitting outside, not really knowing what to do. I felt really bad that we had excluded him. A few of the boys came out and sat with me as I was upset, but Joel was still angry, asking me why I had spoken about money and saying that if we didn't want to do it for them then we shouldn't do it. He said that it made them feel guilty when we spoke about money.

Then things got worse as Matthew (the leader) appeared, obviously having been summoned by someone because of the problem. He saw that I was upset and shouted at Jonah in an attempt to defend me saying, "What's the problem here? Are you causing problems?" and hit him hard on the back. I really felt bad now as the poor boy hadn't had any food and was now being assaulted by an older boy on my behalf! I tried to calm things down and to explain to the boys that I was really just trying to help them, but I got frustrated when they were ungrateful. The following day I apologised to Joel for shouting at him and he accepted this, but our relationship was difficult from then on.

After the incident, we allowed a few extra boys to come, providing they shared the food of our regular boys and that they didn't invite extra people on purpose. We didn't have any further problems in that respect. One of the extra boys, John, turned up on the bridge occasionally, and because I had never seen him before I thought he was new. His English was pretty good, and I could tell he was going to school. He seemed to know the other boys a bit, but I didn't think he was one of them. So when he came up from under the bridge really high one day and fell asleep on the ground near our table, I looked after him and was really worried about him, believing it was his first time inhaling solvents. When he woke up, I gave him a big lecture about drugs, and I also lectured the other boys about getting new people involved and being a bad influence, etc. I later found out that John had already been to rehab for a year and was actually an experienced drug user. I felt pretty stupid.

Mark continued to cause problems, and one day we had gathered the whole group for the evening meal. Mark was in a bad mood and was arguing and demanding things straight away. We went via a clothes shop to buy some new shorts for Reuben, as they had indecent holes in them. Whilst in the shop, Mark deliberately kept trying to attack Adam, a younger boy. He crouched on the ground like a karate expert and I felt afraid, as I knew Mark could really hurt Adam. We tried to stay in-between the two of them, but Mark was intent on having a fight and moved around, trying to take swipes at Adam. I got really angry with him, as he was one of the older boys that we were closer to, and he should've known better.

Outside, Mark stormed off up the street and refused to come back. We let him go, glad to be rid of him until he returned with alcohol and tried to get the others to drink it. We went straight to the feeding venue and banned him from entering unless he ditched the alcohol, which he did. But the incidents with Mark were becoming more frequent, and I still didn't understand him. No amount of reasoning changed his mind if he had decided on a course of action, and he was a really bad influence on the other boys.

We had problems on most days, as we continued to divide the group. We encouraged those who really wanted to change to leave their street family behind and take the opportunity being offered to them. The problem was that because I was the closest to most of them and had spent the most time with them, when they were upset or angry they always targeted me. The targeting was inevitably personal, as they had learned how to upset me. It even continued on Facebook when I was on the ship in the evenings. My support at several stages came from an unlikely source. Paul started defending me, asking Reuben, "Why do you always get mad with Ma'am Natalie?" He also became angry with Simon and told him not to say anything else about me. I think he was fed up with the younger ones complaining and being ungrateful. It was hard for him to stand against them, but his loyalties were changing, and I began to have hope for his future.

CHAPTER TWENTY-ONE

The Worst Day

The worst day of our entire ministry on the bridge was when we took the boys to a park area (Volunteer's Park,) next to the river and were playing games and chatting with them. After a while, we became aware that some of the boys had disappeared and sadly we easily located them sniffing glue in a concealed area nearby. They tried to deny it, but I had seen them doing it. Reuben even joined them after I warned him that he would be excluded from the evening meal. The boys then came out from their location and there was an equal split in terms of who had (Simon, Luke, Joshua, Reuben) and hadn't taken solvents (Joel, Paul, Adam, Mark.)

The ones who had taken the drugs were mingling with the others, but we explained that, because of what they had chosen to do, they weren't allowed to come to the evening meal. Luke became really upset whilst I was talking, and having taken a book out of his pocket, he slowly and deliberately began tearing pages out of it and throwing the pieces into the river. I saw that it was one of our books: *The Greatest Story Ever Told.*

At that point, I told the "good" boys that it was time to leave, as I wanted to get them away from the obvious temptations. I could feel that something was about to boil over as the atmosphere was tense. As we started to leave, the "bad" boys followed us and tried to stop us from leaving. They were blowing solvents in the faces of those who hadn't taken any and were calling us names and using bad words. They were inhaling heavily from bags that they produced from hidden pockets in their clothes. They followed us up the street as we tried to get away.

What happened next reminds me of something from a movie. I told the boys that were drug-free to speed up, so we walked single file at a rapid pace. The boys on drugs rushed along beside us and around the other boys, enticing them to take the solvents and swearing and shouting. Reuben shouted for me to look as he threw the flip-flops I had recently bought him onto the roof of a building. The others copied him and also threw things we had given them on rooftops. The situation was rapidly getting out of control, as the boys were becoming high on the solvents. They blocked our way and deliberately bumped into us as we tried to make good our escape. The local people looked on and wondered what on earth was going on, but maybe due to fear, did nothing to help us.

We were heading for the usual evening meal location, but I knew we would struggle to reach it without serious problems. As we were practically running now, I ran into a man that I knew from a local church, which was en route, and he invited us to take shelter in his church. We followed him, running up the steps and into the main church building where many people were sitting. The other boys chased us up the stairs and squared up to us in the hallway. They were blowing their drugs around and using foul language. The church security officers escorted them outside. I had to specify which boys were with me and which were not. It was really a terrible situation. Outside we could hear them shouting and cursing, and they were specifically shouting personal things about me. We stayed in the church for a while and eventually when we thought it would be safe to leave, we left with some security guards who escorted us across the road to the evening meal.

I was really shaken by what had happened and, as soon as we were inside, the boys appeared at the metal gated doorway shouting obscenities at me. I couldn't look at them so stood with my back to the door. Then it was all too much, and I burst into tears as I stood there, wondering what on earth to do. The good boys ate in silence, as they also hated the division and their loyalties were torn. The bad boys were quieter but blew solvents through the door. When the other boys went over towards them, they waved their hands around and enticed the others, as if they could cast a spell on them saying, "Come and join us, it's fun out here. You know you want to." It was really evil, but the boys inside didn't see it like that. They just thought it was funny and were laughing with them. It was one of the only times where I really felt the presence of evil through these boys and the drugs they were inhaling, and I knew that it was the devil who had hold of their lives.

Paul, at one point, gave some food through the bars to one of them, but we asked him not to do it again. I saw that one of the boys, Simon, wasn't with the others and had left. Reuben was sulking at the back, accusing me of favouritism and saying that my character had changed. He was one of the boys I had a strong bond with, and I definitely didn't want to exclude him. He just couldn't see that it was his own actions that had caused the consequences. The youngest boy, Joshua, was clutching at the bars and really screaming foul language as if he was possessed by something. It was really scary. Zee's father eventually got really angry and shouted at them all to leave. They quietened down but remained outside.

We decided to leave early because of the trouble, but I was worried about how we would get past the boys at the door, especially as they were all now really high on the solvents that they had continued to take whilst outside. As we left, having apologised to the family who were very gracious, we walked single file again down the street. The boys followed us, but they kept punching me in the arm and calling me "ugly." This wasn't the worst thing I had been called, but the repeated punching in the arm became really annoying, as was the way they tried to intimidate us.

When we got nearer to the bridge, I saw Simon sitting with Matthew (the leader.) I spoke to Simon, but he didn't want to talk to me. I wasn't sure if he was ashamed of himself or still angry for being excluded. I told Matthew what had happened, but he already knew as Simon had told him. He got really angry with the boys and shouted at them. Matthew didn't like his boys upsetting us and, if we had real problems, he sorted them out. The younger boys were afraid of him. It was just a shame that he was still inhaling solvents so regularly. We headed back to the ship a bit shell-shocked but sensing that progress was being made in the spiritual battle. We resolved with some hesitation to return to the bridge the following day to do it all again.

CHAPTER TWENTY-TWO

My Favourite Day

We had been praying and hoping that, before the Logos Hope left, the boys would be allowed to visit the ship as one big group. Originally, we were working on a plan to show the Jesus movie in Tagalog down by the bridge, but it just became more and more complicated. In the end, the book-fair manager suggested that we bring the boys to the ship to show them the movie. I asked if they could also have dinner, and it was agreed. We told the boys a few weeks in advance to ensure they made themselves available, and they started to get excited. We made it really clear that any boys who had taken solvents would be excluded with no exceptions. I prayed a lot about it, as I really didn't want to exclude anybody from the big event. We weren't sure how many boys would join us, but I estimated fifteen to twenty based on the numbers we had been seeing on the street on most days. I was sure we would get some extras due to the occasion. We also decided that it would be our last ministry day at the bridge with the book table.

One unexpected problem was that, on hearing the announcement, Simon stated that he wouldn't be able to go to the ship. He would apparently be leaving on November 1st to go home to his family who were going to send him to live with his uncle in a different province so he could return to school. He told us that it was already arranged and that his Dad was going to collect him. I realised that if Simon wasn't going to be able to come to the ship, we would have to do something special for him instead, so I prepared a gift bag for him to take with him with some items from the ship and memorabilia etc. I told him I would give it to him on the morning he was leaving and that we would escort him to the bus station. But, in the run-up to his leaving date, he became more and more upset that he couldn't come to the ship with the others. In the end, he decided that he would go home after the ship visit. It was not the type of decision we wanted to encourage, but we couldn't do anything about it.

On this special day, 9th November 2012, we spent the whole day with the boys in preparation for the evening. We started on the bridge with our table as usual as it was to be our final day of ministry. Simon joined in the spirit of the day by giving local people *Gospels of John* and telling them that Jesus loved them. We played pickup sticks and other games on the ground near to the table. It had been a gift from someone in the UK and we used it a lot. To begin with, I was amazed at how something so simple provided hours of entertainment for the boys. Then I realised that they didn't have any material things of their own, so it was the novelty value. We had also promised them that we would buy all of them "halo-halo" before we left. So, after playing some games and taking them for lunch at the venue, as usual, we purchased approximately fifteen "halo halo's" and they sat on the steps at Volunteer's Park, next to the river, eating them. Even Matthew the leader was there enjoying his "halo-halo." After that, we bought flip flops for all of the boys without shoes so that they would be allowed on the ship.

We then played more games, including tag, which made everyone a bit wild and caused the boys to jump on top of each other and on top of me. Some of the crew just chatted with the quieter boys for the whole afternoon. We brought a couple of Frisbees and a football from the ship and were playing with them but, as we were playing near the river, they frequently ended up in it and the boys had to keep retrieving them. I recall towards the end of our games, Luke, who was fifteen, stripped completely naked with his hands covering his dignity and complaining loudly having been nominated to get the Frisbee. It was a funny sight as he waded naked and still protesting into the dirty water to get the item. However, almost immediately after it was returned another boy had thrown it back in again. Luke refused to go back in as he was already dressed, so eventually, Reuben went in wearing his shorts and also complaining. We ended up losing one of the Frisbees which floated away down the river.

Some of the boys climbed a nearby tree. Others climbed out and along a wall to a crevice on a ledge, where they sat and looked out over the river. I ventured to follow them, which caused great interest amongst the boys who had never seen me do anything like that before. The only problem was Adam followed too closely behind. When I couldn't find a foothold anymore and tried to move back, his foot was in my foothold and I thought I would fall in the river. Paul was watching the whole thing with a perplexed look on his face, as a lot of the time, I was quite serious with them. Yet, before his very eyes, I was climbing a wall and shrieking loudly about the possibility of falling in the river! After a few seconds, Paul snapped out of the trance, smiled and grabbed Adam, who didn't have a clue what was going on or the problem he was causing. He pulled him back and out of my way in the nick of time. On safe arrival back to the river bank, I composed myself and started laughing.

At the appointed time, just eleven boys and some crew were collected by a minibus belonging to the ship. There were meant to be two buses, but one wasn't available, so we all squashed into one and some of the crew had to walk back to the ship. The nice thing was that, although some of the boys we had invited didn't turn up at the meeting point, all of our regular boys were there, including the two Muslims. The boys wouldn't sit still and were jumping around inside the bus because they were so excited. We made them sit down as we went past the security point, otherwise, they might not have been allowed into the ship area. Some of the boys had never entered the area, as they weren't even allowed to cross the bridge from Olongapo into Subic Bay.

In the van, a few of the boys had their hands and T-shirts up over their noses and mouths. I asked what was wrong and Paul indicated that he felt ill due to the air conditioning, which he wasn't used to. Joel also was ill, with the start of a fever that continued for nearly a week, so he wasn't his usual self. On arrival at the ship, the boys wanted to run towards the gangway, but they were stopped and given a short talking to by us about the expected standards of behaviour. They listened, and then promptly disregarded everything we had said.

In the lobby, we wrote down all of their names and gave them badges. Fortunately, many crew members were on hand to assist as we had prepared well for the event and knew that we would need a lot of volunteers to keep control. We tried to split them into groups of three for the initial ship tour, with the inevitable result that they wanted to swap and change groups to be with different friends. Two boys, Paul and Joel, had disappeared and I found them waiting in the clinic to see the nurse, as they weren't feeling well and had been escorted there by a well-meaning crew member. I joined them as the nurse was saying, "I don't really know what we can do here…" So I asked them, "Are you well enough for a tour of the ship?" They said "Yes!" straight away and didn't seem to understand how or why they had ended up in the clinic, so I just took them straight back up to join the others. I commented to the nurse that they were street boys who were used to fighting off various ailments and that they would be okay in due course. She tended to agree.

The tour was amusing, as we tried to have two crew members with each group of three boys. However, the boys kept catching sight of each other from various vantage points on the ship and then running to different decks to try and reunite with their friends. I told my group that they weren't allowed to go to the top deck as it is against the ship rules, but then, out of the corner of my eye, I saw another of the groups of boys already up there and two boys hanging over the railings. I shouted for them to get down and then saw the crew member that was supervising them running across the deck to catch up. They had obviously escaped. This resulted in one of the boys from another group shimmying up a ladder to join them on the top deck, which is definitely forbidden. It was all pretty hectic, but also quite funny as we struggled to maintain control. We took them onto the bridge to try on the captain's hat and have photos taken, and then some of them sat on the deck to watch the sunset. After that, they went to the dining room for juice. The ship juice was made from powder and was brightly coloured, so they all had coloured moustaches around their upper lips as they insisted on drinking more and more of the juice which really tasted bad. It was the novelty value I guess.

After the tour, a ship security person, who will remain nameless, approached me and told me that I needed to keep more control of the boys and that we needed to stick to the "official tour route." I nearly laughed out loud on hearing the absurd suggestion, but just said that we would do our best. It was time for dinner and the chef had prepared rice and other items just for the boys, as rice hadn't been on the menu for that day but most Filipino's eat rice morning, noon and night! The boys were allowed to go to the front of the dinner queues, but needed one crew member each, to assist them in getting their food, as they really didn't know what they were doing. All of the crew were really friendly and helpful. They had heard a lot about the boys and the boys were more than happy to talk to them. Once they had their food, the boys were directed to sit in a reserved area to eat.

At that point, I was made aware of a situation in the lobby area. One of the youngest boys, Joshua, just ten years old, had run away from his tour group and to the exit door leading to the gangway. He was clinging to the door, crying, and refusing to let go. I tried to persuade him to join us and eat, but he refused and became more and more hysterical. Eventually, I obtained translation and it turned out he was afraid that the ship would sail with them all still on-board and that they would then be our prisoners. He was really distraught. It took several people about twenty minutes to convince him that we would not sail with him still on-board and that we were not trying to capture him. Eventually, he went upstairs to eat and that was the end of that.

Whilst they were meant to be eating, the boys kept getting up and walking around the dining room, either to engage other crew members in conversation or to take their chances and conceal various food items in their pockets for later. There was always a reason for them to get up and walk around, and of course heading to the "comfort room or CR" (a term for the bathroom in the Philippines) formed a regular part of their routine. One crew member went to the used clothes store on the ship, known as "Charlie," and collected some items of clothing to replace the ones that were really dirty or torn.

Eventually, it was time to watch the Jesus movie (in Tagalog) in a corner of the dining room. Most of the boys gathered near the front of the screen but some hung back, and Reuben wanted to sit on my lap. This was okay but as the movie started I felt a wet patch seeping through to my trousers, and after my initial surprise, as he was a twelve-year-old, not a toddler, I gratefully remembered the earlier escapades in the river, so I asked someone to get him some dry shorts. The boys generally listened well and watched the whole movie avidly, although a few at the fringes of the group and Joel who still wasn't feeling well, fell asleep. In the middle of the movie, we overheard the following excited whisper coming from the two Muslim boys, Joshua and Luke, who were sitting at the front. Joshua said, "This is the part where Jesus is in the tomb for three days." He remembered this from an Evangecube that some crew members had been using on the bridge to share the Gospel!

After the movie, we let them take some sweets and soft drinks with them, and then we ushered them back down the gangway to the bus. Unbelievably, they were even more lively than on the way there! When we reached the city, we let them all out in an excited mass. They continued to hang on to bits of the bus as we were trying to drive away, and they were shouting and singing. I was glad I wasn't going to have to calm them down.

Although the bridge ministry, in terms of the daily presence of crew members with the book table seeking to share the Gospel, had officially ended, we still went to see the boys regularly and continued our feeding programme twice daily. In the days following the ship visit, we began to see small punnets of jam, butter, and other breakfast spreads, in addition to Logos Hope wristbands, that had obviously been acquired from the ship whilst the boys were in the dining room and book-fair. We accepted it as part of the course and were just grateful that they had been able to come after all the planning.

On reflection, although the event was stressful because I was coordinating everything, the rest of the crew really couldn't have made it easier for me. If I needed anyone to do something, everyone was more than willing, and it was obvious that all of the crew really cared about the street boys. I'm sure the boys could see that as well and knew that the care was despite their bad behaviour. It was a real testimony that everyone on-board was patient and no one got angry with them.

CHAPTER TWENTY-THREE

New Beginnings

On continuing the feeding programme, we took the opportunity to invite the Christian couple, mentioned earlier, to come and see the boys, and also the director of a local Christian children's home. The idea was that, as the boys came off the solvents and started thinking about their lives and futures, they might be willing to study. And they would know that they needed to leave the street in order to do this. We had been preparing them during our ministry and always encouraged them to leave the street, go home, or go back to school. But we recognised that some of them couldn't go home for various reasons, so we wanted to provide an alternative option for them to consider. I was already arranging sponsorship in the UK for them if they left the street.

I wanted Paul and Reuben to go to the children's home as I felt they would be able to deal with Paul's TB issues. I also saw that the two boys were close and almost like brothers at times. I thought that Joel and Adam might be suitable for the Christian couple, but I wasn't sure if they would be willing to consider two boys together as they already had six boys aged sixteen to twenty-one and one girl aged eighteen living with them. I repeatedly told Simon that he should return home to his own family, as he told us that he loved his family, although they were poor. Mark was also told to return home to his family, as we had done everything we could to assist him. I didn't know if we could help Luke and Joshua, the two Muslim boys, at this stage. There was only a limited amount we could do for the older boys, who really just needed to find jobs and stick at them, so we prayed with them to find work.

The Christian couple came and watched the boys playing. They spoke to Joel and Adam and agreed that they would return the following day and that if the boys wanted to go home with them that they could. The family lived in New Cabalan which was up a very steep and long twisting road on the outskirts of Olongapo City. It required two jeepney rides, and about forty-five minutes, to get to their house from the bridge area at a cost of forty pesos return fare. They had been praying as a family about taking in more boys for some time and saw our ministry as God's direction and the right time for them to re-open their home. I was surprised that they would agree so quickly but obviously excited at the prospect of two of our boys having a new home to go to. The director of the children's home also visited and witnessed the boys playing. He said that he would return at a later date for further discussion. He was willing to consider re-homing Paul and Reuben, although he was concerned that Paul had TB and the possible impact on their other children. I was thrilled as everything seemed to be coming together.

The following day, Adam went home with the Christian family, but Joel decided he wanted to stay on the street for a while. We talked with him again, and he said that he would consider going the next day. Joel had developed a high fever after being ill for a few days. It was a part blessing in disguise, as he didn't take any drugs during the period because he felt too ill. We wanted to take him to the hospital, but he refused to go. The Christian couple came back the following day to collect Joel, but at that point, Paul asked me loudly in front of them, "Ma'am Natalie, when am I going to go to the children's home?" I knew that he must be finding it difficult to stay on the street whilst not taking solvents, as it had been three weeks, and I was really proud of him. Immediately after making this statement he turned to the Christian couple and asked, "Will you take three?" They contemplated the request for just a few seconds before answering "Yes." Paul started jumping around and getting excited. They told him that they would come back again the following day to collect him. They took Joel home with them, which was a relief as I knew he would be looked after during his sickness.

Later, and privately, the family told me that they had taken the street boys out for a meal in a restaurant at Christmas time the previous year. They had photos of the occasion and I recognised several of our boys. They had at first been reluctant to take Paul, as they remembered his attitude and behaviour from the Christmas celebration. However, because he had asked them directly, they decided to give him a chance. I tried to reassure them that Paul was changing.

The next day, the couple appeared with Adam who had completely shaved his eyebrows off during a period of non-supervision, which caused a lot of mockery from the other boys! He was bouncing around and looked happy though, and it was a great transformation. One of the most noticeable things was that he was now wearing clothes that actually fit him instead of being three times too big. This was something the family enforced with all of the boys, as a practical demonstration to them, that they were leaving their old street lives behind. It made a big difference to their appearance and made them look like young boys instead of gangsters.

They said that Adam had slept for most of the few days. Paul took him outside for a quiet chat and hounded him with questions about what it was like at the house. When he came back, he asked the Christian couple a series of questions, based on the things he had learned from Adam. As we were leaving the evening meal venue, Paul took his TB medicine out of his pocket. It was quickly removed from him with the comment, "I'll take care of that. You have a mum now." Paul repeated this to himself, "I have a mum now."

I was walking with them and felt elated as we walked down the street to go and buy clothes for him. He was dancing as he walked past the loud music in the street. I knew I would be glad to see the back of the long baggy green T-shirt that I had bought him for ten pesos before. He had asked me to buy him a T-shirt, as his was wet, so I agreed but said it had to be cheap. He found a store where the T-shirts were only ten pesos, so I offered to buy him a few as I was expecting it to be nearer fifty pesos, but he said he only needed one. I noted the change in Paul, as previously he would have been likely to have taken the offer of extra clothes and then sold them. But, the changes meant that he only asked us when he really needed something. There were other occasions when he made sure that we weren't wasting our money on things they didn't need.

I was also looking forward to never again seeing Paul sleeping on the street, curled up in a doorway alone. Paul told us that, the previous year, he had been short but had just suddenly started sleeping thirteen hours a day and then grown really tall. For some reason, I always felt really sad when I saw him sleeping like that. Maybe it was because the other boys mostly slept in groups, but he was often alone. I guess seeing him curled up in a doorway reminded me that he had been cast aside like a pile of rubbish. He slept with his arms wrapped around his head as if to block the world out. There was just something about this combination of factors that really made me sad, and I didn't want to see it again. After he left the street, I saw a boy curled up in a doorway exactly as Paul had done before. I was filled with dread for a few seconds before I remembered it couldn't be him as he was living with the couple.

We went to the clothes store with the Christian family, but whilst we were inside, I saw Mark and Luke suddenly appear outside. They hadn't come to the meal that evening, and they were carrying solvents in plastic bags and were very high. Mark wouldn't speak to me at first and I knew he was angry with us. Then he said that we were trying to split their group up and that we were taking away all of their friends. He was really upset and was crying, as he said Paul was his best friend. Luke was more angry than upset, and also accused us of breaking up their friendship group by removing Paul. The two of them were really a sorry sight as they inhaled the solvents and stumbled around in the entrance to the shop.

Paul eventually came out with the family and looked at these former friends. I wondered what he would do, but I knew it wouldn't be a temptation for him as he had been clean for three weeks and he had a future to look forward to. He walked to Luke and looked at him sympathetically. Then he just touched him on the arm and looked a bit embarrassed for his former friend, especially as they were behaving like this in front of the Christian family. Then he turned around and left them, walking off up the street after the family with a bounce in his step. I stayed with Mark and Luke and, as I watched Paul walk away, it was an emotional moment as he left his old life behind and headed for new things.

CHAPTER TWENTY-FOUR

Division and Destruction

There were now three boys with the Christian family and possibilities for some of the others. We arranged a collection on the ship to build an extension to the family home in order to accommodate the new boys, who had been sleeping in the kitchen. After a while, the extension was completed, adding an extra room and more outside living space to the house.

However, there were massive divisions in our remaining group of boys, and the real trouble makers were actively trying to tear everything down. The following day at lunchtime, Mark was really angry. He deliberately engaged us in an argument, accusing us of taking all of his friends away. He got really upset, and we spent time trying to explain to him that the other boys had no family to go back to. We reminded him that he had a family that he could return to at any time and that this is what he should do. It was hard to be patient with Mark, as I kept remembering that he also claimed he was a born again Christian. Mark was causing us real problems and I was afraid of what he would do. He said that he missed his friends and wanted to go and see them. I told him not to go to the Christian family's house as he would not be welcome there. I also told him that his friends would come and see him when they were ready.

Mark worked himself up into a temper and stormed out of the building, telling Reuben to go with him. Reuben followed as, in their group, the younger boys had to obey the older ones, and Mark had placed his hand on Reuben's neck forcing him to obey. Reuben was uncomfortable with what Mark was doing, but he didn't really have a choice. Mark tried to flag down a jeepney in the street, but they wouldn't take him as his clothes were so dirty. Reuben hung back and I tried to convince him to stay, but I believe Mark had already threatened him as he looked afraid. I told Mark again that he was not to go to the house, and then talked to him and Reuben for a while longer. In the end, I thought I had convinced them not to go. So we went back to the bridge.

Later, when we turned up to the evening meal, Joel and Adam were already there playing pool and Mark was sitting in a chair with a smug expression on his face. I walked straight over to him and told him to leave and that he was not welcome. I knew what had happened straight away and was really devastated at the turn of events, after all the work we had done convincing the two boys to live with the family in the first place. Mark had gone to the house and had taken Joel and Adam away with him. Later, Paul confirmed that this was what had happened and, on further questioning, also confirmed that Mark had offered them all solvents at the house. Paul had declined and stayed at the house alone. Adam hadn't wanted to leave, but Joel persuaded him, as he was bored at the house.

I tried to speak to Joel and Adam, but Joel shouted that they had been told off at the house and that it was boring there. They didn't want to go back. They left together after Mark, who was still hanging around outside. I was so disappointed and upset with Mark. It was one thing for him to make choices about his own life, but he was sixteen and he was dragging the younger boys down with him. The only thing that salvaged the situation slightly was that Paul had remained there and refused the very great temptation offered to him by a former close friend of his.

When the director of the children's home came to visit our boys again, he was immediately concerned about Joel's fever. We explained that we wanted him to go to the hospital, but that he had refused. He asked if there was any other option, and we explained what had happened at the Christian family home. We added that we were trying to persuade him to go back to no avail. I told the director about some of the problems we had been having with Mark, and he asked to have a private word with him. I was surprised but agreed, as by this point we needed any help we could get in dealing with Mark. I was also surprised when Mark agreed immediately to go with him and have a private chat, as I thought he would refuse. The director later said that he would pray for Mark every day for a month. Mark's attitude changed after their chat and, although he had his ups and downs, he didn't try to influence the other boys in a negative way, which is the main thing we had been struggling with. I was really grateful to the director for his intervention and wondered what on earth had been said!

We continued the feeding programme for a short time but found that the remaining boys were no longer serious about leaving the street, and we continued having to exclude some of them for drug use. I was also worried about the impact our ministry was having on Zee's family business as the boys would sometimes attend the premises "out of hours" asking if they could sleep in the doorway and with various other requests. The family dealt with the situation and the requests really well as they had started to love the boys as well. We learned when trying to help the boys that if we drew attention to a particular person or premises it was difficult to put reasonable boundaries in place because the boys were on the street twenty-four-seven with nothing to do. The family didn't complain about any of the problems being caused and persevered with the boys throughout the ministry.

However, due to the problems, we brought the ministry to a close after a few weeks as we were also required elsewhere. After the conclusion of the ministry, Zee's family really missed the boys and often asked how they were doing and sought them out to speak to in the street. During our ministry, they willingly and cheerfully sacrificed their time and home at virtually no notice, diligently collecting the food from the market daily and later preparing it. They even gave the boys vitamins for their health!

Such an example is sadly rare, but for us and the boys it was really a great blessing and the family will receive their reward later in eternity. I believe that although the feeding programme seemed not to have produced the desired outcome with all of the boys leaving the street, it was still the turning point in some of their lives. It was the first time they had been solvent free for more than a few hours and it gave them the chance to think about their lives and futures. Later we asked them why they had cut their drug use down so much and the vast majority of the responses were "because you were feeding us!" This proved definitively that the main reason for their solvent abuse was hunger. The response made the entire trauma worthwhile because we could see that we were slowly making a difference in the lives of the boys and that they were starting to make more sensible decisions.

CHAPTER TWENTY-FIVE

Mixed Emotions

Eventually, we had to bring the bridge and feeding ministry to a close due to work requirements on-board the Logos Hope. Both of my managers had been very flexible and patient for a long time, but the time came when I had to get to grips with my job as administrator of the book-fair. Emotionally, I was totally exhausted and found that, although some tried, people on the ship really couldn't understand what we had been dealing with on the bridge. They told me to try and find a way to "let it all go" emotionally, as we would be leaving imminently, but I wondered what exactly the phrase meant and how to do it. I had seen and been involved in things that had changed my heart forever. I had already decided that I wanted to return to the Philippines in the future, as I felt God's call in my heart and therefore I didn't see the purpose of letting go of what I had already experienced.

I didn't even know where the country of the Philippines was before setting sail on the Logos Hope, so there was no hidden agenda on my part. I also had no idea that I would have a heart for troubled street teenagers because I had no prior experience of the type of work, apart from working for the police in England. Clearly, that was very different as we arrested the troublemakers and put them in a cell for the night. But, I had found myself in a foreign country, at times, protecting the street teenagers from the police and other authorities. What a turn around.

Being removed from the ministry, however, did serve a purpose. It was good at this stage to have an emotional and physical break from the ongoing work with the boys and to do something different. It helped me to gain some perspective and recognise that, even if just one of the boys really changed, it would be a miracle of God. I continued to pray for all of them but knew that my hopes and expectations for many transformed lives may be unrealistic.

Whenever the boys contacted me online whilst I was on the ship, I encouraged them to leave the street and go to the home of the family who had made it clear that they were willing to take any of the boys at any time. The children's home was still an available option, but they were only willing to accept children that were really willing to give everything and that really wanted to leave the street, not those who would keep changing their minds. I couldn't recommend any of my boys anymore, as they continued changing their minds daily.

During this time, I was encouraged that Paul remained at the house, although he was being difficult with the family at times and was extremely stubborn. The family brought him to the ship to visit us and it was really great to see him looking so clean and wearing nice clothes. He was even joking around with us and made the other crew members laugh as he didn't seem to know the correct use of many everyday items. At one point, he did a demonstration of what would happen if he put his hand into an electric socket asking us if it was "ten thousand volts "and then pretending to be electrocuted. I was pleased that he was smiling a lot and seemed relatively happy.

Soon after that first visit, Paul went to the street to find Reuben, and when he was located he encouraged him to join the family. Reuben agreed and went back to the house with him. The arrangement lasted for a while and the two boys came to see us on the ship with the family several times. However, both boys were increasingly stubborn, and Paul often contacted me on Facebook to complain about minor things. Paul became jealous of Reuben because of the attention he was getting from the family, who seemed to like him more. The family admitted that they struggled with Paul because he was difficult and that they thought Reuben was funny, but I don't think they showed excessive favouritism. Paul just needed that extra bit of attention and reassurance.

I went out for the evening with the family and the two boys and I could see that Paul was really unhappy. He refused to speak to me for the whole evening. The family managed to resolve things, but I was upset by Paul's attitude as I was trying to help him. One of the things which I found really hard was that the boys constantly spoke about returning to the street and used it as a threat a lot of the time to get their own way. It was emotionally tough as I couldn't bear the thought of them being back on the street, but I couldn't allow them to walk all over us either. The threats to run away became reality several times as the boys jostled for the first position in the household, but I told them to go back to the house and apologise, which they did at first.

Only a week after Paul and Reuben had joined the family, Simon also asked if he could join them and the family agreed. We had previously told Simon that he should go home to his own family, but as he obviously wasn't going to do this, it seemed better for him to go to a different family than to be on the street. They took to Simon instantly since he was better behaved than the other two and polite. At this time, we decided to buy a special present for each of the boys at the house. We also obtained some books from the ship and other cheap gifts from Olongapo to try and give them extra things to do and to encourage them not to run away. We gave Paul a cheap cell phone with a camera, Reuben a skateboard, and Simon a bike. The gifts later caused problems as Mark forced Paul to give him his cell-phone and then sold it, Reuben didn't know how to use the skateboard and wanted a cell-phone instead, and the bike broke. However, for a while, they enjoyed their gifts, and the initial excitement when they first received them was really great to see.

The three boys came to the ship several times with the family, but almost always got into some sort of trouble because they kept running around. I offered to take the boys around the ship for a tour, but when we began they were really naughty. They ran away from me and took things in the dining room. They wouldn't listen to anything I said and kept walking off. Paul ran away down a flight of stairs, only returning after about ten minutes. I was really angry due to the security lapse, which could potentially get me into trouble, so I told him off. I dragged him and the other boys back through the door to where the family was waiting and told them what had happened.

The family told them off and said they needed to apologise to me, but it is really hard for a Filipino child (more so than in a Western country,) due to it being a shame culture.

They began to say one by one that they wanted to go back to the street rather than face me and apologise. I couldn't believe it, surely a simple apology wasn't too much to ask, but they would rather jeopardise their opportunity to stay with the family. I asked them how they thought the family felt every time they made their threats in an attempt to hurt me. Eventually, all three boys apologised but it was hard work! I then took them on another tour, which was much more civilised, but I realised that they still hadn't made definite decisions to stay off the street so I lived in constant fear of them running away.

CHAPTER TWENTY-SIX

My Big Mistake

Joel asked me one day if I could take him to visit the other three boys at the house. The family obviously didn't want him living there again. (You will recall that Joel and Adam ran away from the family home within two days of their arrival after Mark took solvents to the house.) The family also said later that, whilst Adam was at the house, he had been caught smoking and rummaging through someone else's pockets in one of the bedrooms. It was Joel who had persuaded Adam to leave, but the family didn't want either of them back. Joel had been good for a few days, was pleading with me, and seemed just to want to see his friends. I decided it would be okay as deep down I felt sorry for him. It was a big mistake.

When we got to the house, Joel said sorry to the family for running away and for his previous attitude. They forgave him straight away and said he could stay again if he wanted to and he agreed. They really were very gracious towards him in light of what he had done. But, despite Joel's apologies and promises, there was a lack of real sincerity and it was clear that things weren't right. Shortly after we arrived, there was an atmosphere of trouble. Joel encouraged Reuben to smoke, and Paul started a fight with Reuben after getting angry about something then hit him really hard.

Things all calmed down and the boys went to play basketball nearby. However, when we went to call them for dinner, they began walking hurriedly away from us. When we speeded up to catch them, they started running with Joel at the helm. All of the boys followed Joel and started running off down the main road back towards

Olongapo City. I was angry with Joel as we pursued them as I realised I shouldn't have trusted him or taken him to the house. We shouted for them to come back and followed for a while, heading along the highway. Paul stopped running and turned and looked at us, seemingly caught in a dilemma, but he came to the right decision and began walking slowly back towards us. He came back to the house with us, but Reuben and Simon had left with Joel, I really couldn't believe it! We then broke the news to the family. They took it quite well, but I felt really bad as I knew Joel had deceived me. Later I asked Joel why they had run and he said it was because we were chasing them!

After a few days, the family were in a jeepney in the city when they saw Reuben being chased by DSWD staff. They called his name and he ran and jumped into the jeepney with them, as an alternative to being sent to rehab. We also located Simon and Joel one morning asleep on some cardboard. As we approached them, Simon woke up but Joel remained asleep. We had been worried for some time about the influence of Joel on the other boys. It was clear that, even though they were a similar age, Joel was the leader of the younger group and they were afraid of him. We heard stories of him slapping them whilst they were asleep and stealing their money. We told Simon that it was his opportunity to leave Joel asleep and go back to the family. I didn't really think he would do it, but immediately he got up and said, "Let's go now." So we quietly ushered him away from the sleeping Joel. This particular incident was amusing, as it felt like we were stealing something or doing something we shouldn't, but really it was ridiculous. We shouldn't have been afraid of Joel, a twelve-year-old boy.

Having sneakily returned Simon to the house without Joel's knowledge, he ran away again only a day or so later and only agreed to go back if he could take another Muslim boy Joshua with him. The family agreed to take both of them, and so ended up with four of our street boys. I warned them that Joshua had stolen from me before, but it seemed to be a good solution for him to keep him off the street. We were told later, by some former neighbours of Joshua's family, that we should keep Joshua safe to protect him from his family who were cruel.

I asked a local church leader if he would check up on Luke (the other Muslim boy) for us and visit his family when the ship left, as he was the only boy we really hadn't been able to offer proper help. I had been in discussions with the director from the children's home about Luke because they said they had had Muslim residents before and that it wouldn't necessarily be a barrier. But eventually Luke's family moved to Manila and we didn't see him again. I spoke to him a few times online when he first moved and he said that he still wasn't going to school and that he wanted to return to Olongapo. I didn't hear from him again after that.

As the ship was preparing to leave Subic Bay, Joel and Adam were the only two boys left on the street from our original group. Joel contacted me online after a while and said that he really wanted to change his life so I went to speak to them in the city. When I found them, they were doing paid work and weren't really interested in talking to me, so I left. This often happened. The boys said one thing online and, when I tried to speak to them, they had forgotten because they were high on solvents at the time or had changed their minds.

Before the ship left I had a final conversation with Joel. He was sitting on the ground with a whole gang of younger boys. He was obviously miserable, as his friends of the same age were now living with the family, forcing him to hang around with younger children. However, persistently stubborn, he said that the group hadn't needed our help in the first place and that all we had done was destroy their friendships. He accused me of favouritism saying, "It's okay because I know you never really liked me or Adam in the first place." I told him that wasn't true at all, that it was due to their behaviour that they had had problems and reminded him that they had had the same opportunities as the other boys. He spoke of another girl from the UK that had helped them once. He said that he knew that she was the only one who loved them and cared for them. It hurt me to see him like this, but I couldn't give him another chance with the family, because I couldn't risk jeopardising the other boys at the house, so I had to just leave him on the street, which was really hard.

Overall, I was happy, as all of our boys had been given an opportunity to leave the street if they wanted, and this had been one of our main goals. All four boys wanted to stay with the family and were adapting to family life as the ship was about to leave. However, the incidents of running away and returning continued and we found ourselves almost daily having to take one boy or another back to the family after various disputes.

The problem was that the bonds between the boys were so great. We were constantly fighting for control and to separate them from the only family they knew, their street family, because of the negative influence they had on each other. It was an emotional rollercoaster for me. The elation of getting one of the boys to leave the street, only to find a few days later that he had run away again, was very hard to cope with. I knew that the boys would only truly change if they made the decision to leave the street themselves rather than being put under pressure, but it was hard to watch them making bad choices and then suffering the consequences.

CHAPTER TWENTY-SEVEN

Final Farewells

The family visited the ship a few times with all four boys, even bringing them to a Sunday church service on-board. During the service, three of the boys promptly fell asleep, lounging all over the chairs. They only woke up for the singing, joining in loudly and out of tune. In the service, Paul drew something on a piece of paper and afterwards I read what he had written: "Jesus loves Paul", "I love you Lord", "Paul loves Jesus and Natalie", "God is my guide", and other similar things. I photocopied the page, as it was such an encouragement from one of our toughest street boys.

We visited the boys at the family house several times, including the day before we were due to leave with the ship. We had a great time messing around and laughing with the family. Whilst we were eating, I told Reuben that he needed to eat more because he was a growing boy. Simon helpfully translated for him, but everyone burst out laughing. He had translated my comment as "She thinks you are very wise because you have a big head." Then Paul told me off for leaving rice on my plate, as leaving food was against the house rules. I acknowledged this, as I wanted to be a good example to him, and told him it was the same at my house in England.

Later Paul was joking around and kept grabbing me and putting my hands behind my back in a police move that I had foolishly taught him before. Then he said "Police arrest" and refused to let me go as I struggled for freedom. Everyone else thought it was hilarious as I was screaming from being tickled. I was a bit worried. I knew I shouldn't have taught the boys things like this in case they used them on other people and really hurt them.

As we were leaving the house for the last time, Paul asked me for one of my wristbands with the Bible verse "With God all Things Are Possible." Matthew 19 vs 26. I gave him a blue one, but he gave it back to me and asked for the black one I was wearing. Then he told me that when I came back to the Philippines we could swap back. I knew this was his way of reminding me that I had promised to return. I said "Ingit ka" as I left which I thought meant "Take care", but he looked confused and started laughing and repeating it. It actually means, "You are jealous." I should've said, "Ingat ka!"

The following day, December 11th, 2012, the family brought the boys to the shipyard to say goodbye to us, as it was to be our last day in port. All four boys were looking well but sad that we were leaving. The other crew members and some local people were really amazed at the transformation as they saw the boys playing on the quayside and recognised them from the street in Olongapo. Later Paul, unaware that he was being observed, played a game with a small boy on the quayside. He covered up his eyes and pretended to be crazy, then went back to normal. The small boy was giggling and they were repeating this again and again. I thought back to when we had first met Paul, what a different boy he had turned into!

After that, I was sitting on the quayside, with some crew members, on a stack of wood quite high off the ground when Paul approached me and grabbing my legs said: "Ma'am Natalie, I will miss you so much." Unfortunately, this caused me to lose my balance and fall forward off the pile landing with my bare feet very close to some metal spikes protruding upwards from the ground. I just crouched there for a few seconds feeling thankful for the exact final positioning of my feet!

Reuben was sulking and kept looking up at the ship, shaking his head, and looking really miserable. I knew it was because we were leaving and I felt sad for him. Later, the boys trailed home after the family as we said goodbye for the last time.

Once they had gone and I was back inside the ship, a Filipino crew member approached me to tell me about a conversation she had been having with one of the boys outside. The boy was talking enthusiastically about wanting to study and to get on with his life and other things. I knew she was talking about Paul, and hearing what he had said made me cry, because of everything I had been through with him on the street and because I knew that, out of all the boys, he was really serious about wanting to change. I knew I would miss the boys when we left but I thought that was the end of the emotional goodbye. Not so.

A few hours later, whilst I was in the queue for dinner, I heard my name being paged to contact the gangway. Everyone in the queue looked at me surprised. Shore leave (permission to leave the ship to go on-shore) had already been withdrawn as the ship was about to leave, so it wasn't a good time for visitors! When I went to the gangway and looked out, there were Paul, Reuben and Joshua again. I just stood at the top of the gangway and put my head in my hands as I asked myself whether I could go through the emotional drama all over again, but I couldn't just leave them there. I asked for permission to go down the gangway, which was granted. I went to hug the boys and say goodbye again. I couldn't understand why they had returned, as I had seen them leaving with the family earlier, but now they seemed to be unsupervised.

They said Simon had already run away from them, throwing his shoes in the air and shouting that he was returning to the street. One down before we had even left! I made all three remaining boys look me in the eyes, promise to stay at the house, to be good, and to study hard. They all did so, but I knew it wouldn't hold them to anything. After a while, they left because it was getting late. In the end, the ship didn't leave until the following day. I was half expecting to look out of the window and see them on the quayside again or to be paged in the middle of the night to go to the gangway. I would gladly have stayed behind. The next few months were to be very difficult.

When the ship sailed away from Olongapo, I knew I had left part of my heart behind. It wasn't so much about the place, but about the boys whom I had come to know and love. I knew that some of them didn't have anyone who really cared for them and that, for a time, I had been that person. I hoped and prayed that they would remember that Jesus loved them more than me and that they would look to Him after I had gone.

Simon did go back to the house temporarily, after contacting me on Facebook and saying he was sad. The family arranged private tutoring for all four boys together, but they had just two lessons before things went wrong. It seems Joshua wanted to speak to the tutor about something, but she was busy with one of the other boys and he didn't want to wait, so he shouted for attention. When this didn't work he flew into a rage, screaming, shouting, and threatening to burn down the church where they were holding the lessons and to smash all of the windows. He then ran off, followed by Simon who said he was going to get him back.

After a few days on the street, Simon and Joshua returned to the family together. They were dirty, tired, and hungry, but a few days later they ran away again, each time with new clothes and shoes that the family had generously given them. Shortly after the last incident, Joshua's Muslim family moved to Manila. I haven't had any contact with Joshua since, although I have been told he is back in Olongapo City.

I remained in daily contact with the Christian family via email and Facebook. But I was constantly receiving messages from the boys to say they were running away or were sad, which was playing havoc with my emotions. The boys told me their complaints online but I couldn't do anything about it because we were now in a different country. In the end, I had to discipline myself not to check my Facebook account regularly because I couldn't deal with the ups and downs of the boys' lives.

By Christmas time 2012, just two weeks after the ship had left Olongapo, Paul was the only boy left at the house. The others had run away. The family were especially worried about Simon, as there had been an indication that he had some kind of health problem and he wasn't looking well when they had last seen him.

Reuben left because he didn't like the house rules and wanted to play outside at night. The family obviously didn't allow that, so he just stopped going home. He ate regularly at a neighbour's house, but eventually, the neighbour said to him, "Why are you here? You're not part of this family." The rebuke upset him so he went back to the Christian family home for a while. He then got involved in a fight with a gang in the area and threw a rock at the head of one of the gang leaders. They threatened to kill him if he ever came back to their area. The family tried to smooth things over to no avail. He was like a wandering animal with nowhere to call home. When I heard the story, I immediately thought back to the gang fight, with the students, many months before, and was relieved that I had intervened, as the latter incident proved that Reuben would quite happily have thrown a rock at one of the students that day.

After New Year, Paul left the house twice after arguments, and on one occasion returned having taken solvents and was therefore told to leave again. However, in early February, he left after another argument and was caught the same day by the DSWD staff who by this point had obtained a court order for him to go to rehab. It seems they had been holding off enforcing the order whilst he was living with the family but his unwise decision to leave had consequences. He was quickly transferred on 6th Feb 2013 to rehab in Manila which effectively put a temporary end to everyone else's efforts to help him.

CHAPTER TWENTY-EIGHT

Rehab

A couple of months passed and many teams were preparing to head out from the ship during the April 2013 dry dock in Hong Kong. Quite a few of the teams being sent out were also going to the Philippines. I requested to be part of a team going to Olongapo, praying that if it was right I would get it. Although I had decided a few months before that I would return to the Philippines after I finished my commitment with the ship, I had started to doubt my decision during my absence from the country and needed confirmation of my calling. I was hoping a return would provide it. If I returned to the Philippines, I prayed that I would just know if it was right. The teams were assigned and I was allocated to a Philippines team, but to Manila instead of Olongapo. At first, I was disappointed, but then I realised that I might be able to visit Paul and Adam in rehab (Adam had been transferred there after being picked up by the DSWD in March.)

I was assigned to a team of six heading to a poor area of Manila for the month. When I looked at the map, I saw that it was just one hour away from the rehab facility. It was a big thing to ask my team leader and the host of the church we were staying in if I could take a day out to visit the boys. However, when I explained the situation, they were more than happy to let me go on one Saturday and even provided me with a translator from the church. So, we set off, not really knowing exactly how to get there, but eventually arriving safely at the rehab centre in Manila.

The centre is primarily for adult rehabilitation, but they also house sixty to eighty children from ages eleven to eighteen. The rehab is the only government institution in the entire area that houses the children. DSWD's from miles around obtained court orders to send their problem "rugby boys and girls" there. Olongapo was one of the most distant provinces to send children to the centre, which caused its own problems. The boys were transferred from their local province en masse and then spent a minimum of eight months being rehabilitated and going to school at the centre. Sometimes they were neglected or forgotten by their own DSWD, (out of sight out of mind), but this DSWD remained responsible for their welfare, including providing clothing and toiletries because the centre itself didn't have a budget for these items. This is just one of the unworkable rules that I encountered.

The security at the centre was tight and very similar to a prison, with many guards, searches on entry, and lists of banned items including Mentos and full-length toothbrushes. Bizarrely, with the latter item, they snapped them in half, which seemed to create more of a weapon than before if that was what they were worried about. There was also a strict dress code. In fact, if you turned up wearing trousers that had a two-inch gap at the bottom where your ankles are, you would be refused entry. The reason for the code was less clear, as the inmates wore shorts.

In the Philippines, many security and legal procedures appeared to have been copied from the West, but as the purpose behind the procedures was sometimes not known or was interpreted incorrectly, the things became unnecessarily inflexible and bureaucratic. The officials almost always stuck to their brief, even if it didn't make sense or was not fit for purpose. There were few opportunities to complain and things were rarely addressed effectively or changed if you did. It was just part of life but could be frustrating, especially when you are not trying to do anything illegal and are just trying to help people.

On my first visit, after going through security and other bits and pieces, myself and my translator, were ushered to a large open area with tables and asked to wait for a while. Then, a social worker came and asked for the names of the boys that I wanted to see. I listed all of the boys that I knew, in case there were others somehow there, but I really was only expecting to see Paul and Adam.

After waiting for a while, I saw them coming towards me and, the biggest surprise of all, Joel was with them! I was saddened by their appearance, their heads had all been shaved and they looked thin and miserable. They huddled together in a small group as if they would find safety in numbers and they were herded by some older boys. They looked dazed, confused, and very lost. Joel burst into tears when he saw me, and he and Adam both came over straight away and hugged me. Paul also struggled not to cry, as I tried to hold my own emotions in check, as I knew it was important for them that I remained in control. I was so surprised to see Joel, who had only arrived three days before my visit. All hostilities from before were completely forgotten. I couldn't really speak much Tagalog, so I just asked them what they were doing and they said they were cleaning every day and were very unhappy.

We sat for a few hours chatting and ate some snacks we had brought for them. I also brought Bibles, many children's books, toiletries, clothing, and other items which they were very excited about. Interestingly, the thing that Paul and Joel were most concerned about was that their Facebook profiles might be deleted due to inactivity on their accounts. I was incredulous when they mentioned this, as it would have been the least of my priorities in a place like rehab. It again demonstrated their immaturity in setting priorities and reminded me that they were just children. I agreed to hack into their accounts using the passwords they supplied, just to keep their accounts active but thought they would forget about it in time. On subsequent visits, the subject was mentioned several times. I was reluctant to hack into Paul's account because previously he had had a disgusting pornographic image as his cover photo. I had refused to become friends with him until it had been removed. After initially claiming he didn't know how to change it, he had succumbed when my friendship became more important than his street credibility. Joel had created a wanted poster of himself with the caption "Wanted: Dead or Alive" as his profile picture, which was less offensive.

The boys asked for some other things too and, as there was a small shop within the rehab compound, I bought them everything they needed, which wasn't a huge amount in monetary terms. I was desperate to try and improve their lives a little, but I was irritated by the attitude of the guards manning the shop who kept trying to get me to buy more and more items. They suggested to the boys that they might need various items that they clearly didn't.

The boys told me that Adam had already been in trouble for fighting and that they had had no other visitors. They told me too that there were some boys and girls with them who had no visitors for their entire year at the centre, which really made me sad. I determined to try and change this. We finished our visit after a few hours and said goodbye. I promised to visit again when I was able, but I wasn't sure when this would be as the ship's schedule was still unclear and subject to change. I remained cheerful until we got outside but then was in a daze for the rest of the day, appalled at what I had seen.

Thinking about the situation at the rehab later, I thought how terrible it must be for children of this age to be in a prison type of environment, far away from everything they knew with no friends or family to visit them. The boys that did have families in Olongapo wouldn't get visits as their families wouldn't be able to afford to travel to see them. It was one of the main reasons for them being on the street in the first place: Poverty. It was a vicious circle. At first, I felt completely helpless as I didn't see what I could do, so I spent the next few days crying every time I thought about the boys alone there without any friends or visitors. After a few days, I contacted the Christian family and asked them whether they would be willing to visit the boys once a month in the centre if I arranged to fund the visit. They agreed to the idea almost immediately and I was just so grateful. But it didn't help the rest of the boys and girls who were there.

I wondered about mobilising local churches into some kind of visitation scheme to encourage long-term relationships with some of the children without family members. But I knew it would be a lot to ask the local community, especially as I had no contacts or connections in the area. There was also the issue of confidentiality of the children to contend with, and the fact that some were from other faiths. It was just the beginning of an idea that might also help to solve the problem of the children leaving rehab and going straight back to the street afterwards. It was really a big problem. The government spent a lot of money rehabilitating the children for a year and then some of them were ending up back in rehab for the following school year, having only just been released, because the underlying causes of their solvent abuse hadn't been addressed. They returned to problem families and abusive home situations in many cases. I thought that maybe it would make a difference if they had a more stable connection with a Christian on the outside.

I started by writing a letter to the DSWD head office for the area and also to the governor of the rehab. I requested permission to begin a visitation scheme by mobilising local churches. I explained in the letter how I would deal with the confidentiality and other faith issues, and how the scheme would benefit the children. I waited several months but didn't receive an official response. Eventually, I received verbal permission from the governor at the rehab, but nothing from DSWD. It was difficult to do anything with the idea at this stage as I was back on the ship and we had moved to Hong Kong, so the idea was put on the back burner.

CHAPTER TWENTY-NINE

Bonus Visit

Originally, before the very long dry dock in Subic Bay in 2012, the Logos Hope had been due to visit several other ports in the Philippines. Due to the extension, the ports had been postponed to a later date. It was now decided we would visit the additional ports of San Fernando and Puerto Princesa. This was a great surprise as I had thought the ports had been cancelled and, due to the amount of time we had already spent in the Philippines, I didn't think we would spend any further time there especially not so soon after leaving. The ship's community was divided over the decision with half of the crew wanting to go back as they had developed a heart for the country, and the other half never wanting to see the place again, even on a map. The trauma of the conditions some had experienced during the long dry dock resulted in some strong views on the subject. It was at this point also that some people's true motivations for being on-board were exposed as they complained that they were not experiencing enough different cultures or countries!

We arrived in San Fernando in the Philippines on May 24th, 2013, and I immediately made plans to visit Olongapo and the boys in the rehab in Manila eight hours away! We only had a two-week window of opportunity because Puerto Princesa, our subsequent port, was on a separate island and required a flight to reach Manila or Olongapo. We were allocated just seven days holiday a year whilst on the ship. I had saved most of mine having only taken a few days off when my parents had visited, so I had plenty of capacity in this respect. I was disappointed not to be able to practice my Tagalog in San Fernando as the people spoke a different language.

My friends and former bridge personnel, Arlene and Nick, also wanted to see the boys in rehab, so we travelled together on various buses and public transport for eight long hours to reach Manila. We stayed for a few days and went to the rehab on Saturday, meeting the Christian family at the centre.

The boys were very excited to see all of us, as they hadn't been told in advance that we would be visiting and I had told them I probably wouldn't be able to visit again until after I had left the ship. All three boys were still subdued but seemed to have recovered from the initial shock of being in the rehab. They all had scabies though, which hadn't been evident before. Rampant scabies was to be a recurring problem for the boys and for the centre, who couldn't afford to effectively treat them. I made a big fuss about it in the medical centre because I hated to see the boys with open sores and wounds and constantly scratching. But there were no easy solutions.

Another issue for Paul was that, before he went to the rehab, we had been working on getting his teeth fixed. His front teeth were all missing, having rotted away, which he said was from eating too much candy. We had paid for all of the rotten teeth to be extracted, and he had been just about to have his new plate of teeth fitted when he got sent to rehab. Now, he was understandably complaining that he was unable to eat properly, having had so many teeth removed. I went to the health centre within the rehab compound with him and discussed this with a dentist. They didn't think it would be possible to sort his problem out at the rehab although we offered various options to them. We suggested we could pay for Paul to be taken outside with an escort from the rehab to visit a local dentist. In the end, it was agreed that we would take a mould of his teeth and have the new ones created outside.

In reality, this didn't happen, so Paul remained at the centre with no teeth for the duration of his time in rehab. It reminded me of a time on the street when he said, "Ma'am Natalie, give me one hundred million pesos." I replied, "What do you need the money for?" with no response from him. Then, he asked me for other amounts of money which I also refused until finally he grinned at me with the big gap where his teeth should have been very visible and said, "Ma'am Natalie….give me….teeth." which made me laugh.

It was also during the second visit that Paul asked me to be his petitioner (legal guardian.) In practice, I was already sharing this role with the Christian family by attending to his health and medical needs. But I knew that I had to decline his request for several reasons. It wasn't clear whether he had biological relatives that could assume the role. There was a suggestion that he had a grandma somewhere who was still interested in caring for him. I was also not sure exactly when I would return to the Philippines and where in the Philippines I would be based. I was obviously not Filipino and only spoke very basic Tagalog. Being single, in addition to everything else, I felt that it would be the wrong thing to do.

However, I knew the underlying reason for the question. He wanted some kind of reassurance that I was not just going to disappear back to the UK, never to return, and that someone else in his life who he had started to trust would, therefore, turn out to be a fake. I also knew that I must give him this reassurance and that it was a serious matter for him. I told him that I would always be in his life in some capacity and that I would ensure that he was cared for and looked after. I also told him that I loved him and all of the other boys and would do what I could to help them. This seemed to satisfy him.

The boys told us that all of the things we had given them on the previous visit, with the exception of the Bibles, had been stolen by the other boys at the centre, and that it had caused some fights. They quoted some Bible verses from memory, which was encouraging. The reason for the problems was that they hadn't been allocated any storage space to put anything in. The lack of even basic supplies in the sleeping area meant that all of the boys were desperate for things like soap and toothpaste. Again, I purchased the things they asked for in the canteen area, including basic footwear and shorts and T-shirts. The clothing was required to be worn as a uniform, but the centre didn't have a budget for them, so the boys had to purchase them themselves! They all wore borrowed clothes, which they said they had to return, and some of their clothing had holes in it. One of the boys had a twisted wire in the bottom of his shoe to hold it together. All of the boys were complaining that they couldn't sleep properly because they were all in one big room on the floor with no bedding. They said that the room was dirty, resulting in scabies taking up residence.

We gave all of the supplies to the social worker on the second visit, to prevent thieving. Then she asked me whether, instead of just helping our boys, we could find a way to help all of the children at the centre. I felt a bit helpless when she made the request and explained that, as we were missionaries from the ship, we didn't really have the funds for this type of thing, but I said that I would do what I could. She just smiled at me patiently and I left feeling convicted.

Afterwards, I really felt angry that a government centre would house children in these conditions without basic cleaning products, and without proper access to medical and health facilities. Over time, I was often asked for "donations" to buy basic products for the centre like a cleaner for the rooms and rubbish bags. I had to weigh each of the requests individually and make decisions based on how necessary the items were for the wellbeing of the children. To begin with, I said, "I'm not going to purchase these items because it's the government's responsibility and it will just encourage them not to budget for the things next year."

However, after a while, when the things were not purchased if I didn't donate them, I wondered whether there really was an issue with money. Of course, the real problem was the corruption at the top of the chain but, ultimately, by refusing to help the government staff at the centre, I was actually refusing to help the children who were the ones that suffered. So, I became more willing to help, even if it was someone else's responsibility.

CHAPTER THIRTY

Good News and Bad News

After the rehab visit, we went to Olongapo for a brief stay of only two days. Due to the short duration, the three of us rushed around to meet people and to try and find the remaining boys that were still on the street. We located Simon one day, and I was shocked by his altered state. I had been warned by the family that he wasn't well and they had been trying to get him to go to the hospital. He had lost a lot of weight and was limping badly. His eyes were dull and dead and he just looked ill. He came rushing to us and gave me a hug, but I just couldn't believe his appearance. I was really upset, especially when he couldn't catch his breath when he was talking to me and I could hear some kind of wheezing. I told him that he needed to go to the hospital with us right away, but he didn't want to. Reuben was similarly dirty but seemed livelier. He didn't want to speak to me and just stayed away from us. I had been close to him so it upset me, but there wasn't time to really find out what the problem was.

Later as we were walking with Simon and Reuben, we met Mark's mum working and she seemed really happy. She told us that Mark had finally re-enrolled at school for his final year of high school and that he had also enrolled his sister. He was going to school, living back at home, and there were no longer any problems. I was really amazed but thankful that at least one of the boys had changed.

Later Mark was summoned and came to see us, and he really was different. He was very quiet and shy. He seemed almost embarrassed by our presence, but it was clear he wanted to see us. I asked him about the solvents and he said, "I don't want to do that anymore."

Although I was really pleased for him, I couldn't help thinking about the younger boys that he had led back to the street. We knew that he wasn't really addicted to the solvents, as he was only taking them for a short duration and that he could stop at any time. My concern was for the others that he had led astray. Of course, I didn't mention that to him. I knew that he had been desperately unhappy when making these mistakes and I believed that everyone deserved another chance if they sincerely decided to sort things out. I encouraged him to continue what he was doing, as he said he was also going to church and Bible study.

Matthew had moved in with Mark's family and was also living at their house. Although this was to be of short duration, it was good news because Matthew really didn't have a suitable family of his own. Matthew was working, helping Mark's mum, and Mark's dad was also coming home imminently from his work abroad. I was encouraged to hear all of their news.

Before we left late in the evening, we managed to persuade Simon to attend the hospital with the Christian family. However, when they returned, their expressions were sombre. There was something wrong with Simon's heart and he needed to have further tests. They had arranged an appointment at the clinic near the bus station for the following morning, just before we had to leave to travel back to the ship. I didn't think there was any way that Simon would attend the appointment.

The next day we hurried to the bus station and were relieved to see that Simon and Reuben were sleeping on the chairs outside the clinic. I was amazed until Reuben informed us that he had been instrumental in making sure Simon kept to his appointment because he was worried about him. We left Simon having his tests with the family and travelled the eight long hours back to the ship.

Later it was confirmed that Simon had an enlarged heart, probably due to his abuse of solvents, and that he needed to take daily medication, perhaps for the rest of his life. If he didn't take his medication and continued inhaling solvents it would likely be fatal for him. The news was really devastating. To begin with, Simon agreed to go home with the family to try and get better and have his treatment. Reuben encouraged him to go with them but refused to go himself.

CHAPTER THIRTY-ONE

Logos Hope Returns

When we got back to the ship there was a rumour circulating that there was a problem with the engine again and that maybe we wouldn't be able to travel to our intended destination of Puerto Princesa. The director indicated that we might have to travel to another unnamed port in the Philippines that was closer to hand. People began whispering as the director tried not to smile as he knew the impact his announcement would have. Subic Bay and Manila were mentioned as everyone wildly speculated about where it would be. I thought that the director wouldn't allow us to return to Subic Bay due to the psychological impact it might have on some of the crew members who had suffered greatly during the dry dock. In fact, most people didn't want to go back and there were just a few of us that did. I just prayed that God's will would be done. When it was finally confirmed after a few days that we were heading for Subic Bay I was astonished, and I kept thinking the plan would be changed again. Crew members congratulated me as if I had had some personal success as they knew about our ministry to the street boys. I couldn't stop smiling.

On June 11th, 2013, I woke up late and looked out of the window expecting to see unfamiliar surroundings, as the leadership had told us we would be in a different berth to the previous one. But we were in exactly the same berth as before! It was totally surreal. I immediately arranged to visit the Christian family and was one of the first people down the gangway. I saw another crew member running outside and kissing the ground. This was a bit over the top for me, but I knew how he felt. It felt like we were arriving home. The only annoying thing was that we had travelled for eight hours each way to get to Olongapo and Manila just a week before. But it didn't really seem to matter in the big scheme of things. It was unclear how long we would be staying in Subic for, but it wasn't going to be just a few days stop over.

I spent a lot of time walking around Olongapo City trying to find the boys. The former large group of "rugby boys" under the bridge were noticeable by their absence and it was commented on by other crew members. The city was almost eerily quiet as I walked the streets. Previously, I hadn't been able to walk more than a few feet without hearing "Ma'am Natalie" in an excited voice from one direction or another before any number of boys descended on me. The lack of attention was bittersweet because I knew that some boys had left the street to go back home or back to school or were working. But, I also knew that a few were still out there and had been driven underground by our activity and that there were still others in rehab as a last resort.

One unintended, but mostly positive, side effect of our work with the boys was that during and after our ministry, the DSWD and police seemed to step up their activity and efforts to get the boys off the street. I cannot definitively say whether it was due to the heightened visibility of the boys because of our interest in them or just a coincidence in timing. Once the large group had been reduced to twos and threes the peer pressure problem became much smaller and easier for the authorities to manage effectively. This, in turn, made it harder for us to locate the boys as they no longer had the safety of the large group and were often hiding from the authorities. It wasn't as much fun for the boys to hang around all day with one or two others, and they quickly ran out of ideas to keep themselves occupied. They also started to have nagging doubts about their lifestyle choices, knowing that some former street friends were now back with their families and in school. They began to wonder if they would be "left behind." I preyed on their insecurities, for their own benefit, of course, advising them that they would be "left behind" and alone as their friends headed for better things. I encouraged them to take the opportunities being offered to them as they wouldn't be available forever.

On one such occasion, I tried to persuade Timothy a fourteen-year-old former "rugby boy" that I knew, to leave his very low paid job selling toys at the market, for a place in a Christian children's home and the chance of an education. The placement had already been arranged for him as the home were caring for his younger brother. As I was speaking, an older man happened to pass by and caught the gist of the conversation. To my surprise, as Filipino's tend to be shy especially in the presence of foreigners, the man intervened and began advising Timothy in strong terms that he should "grab the opportunity being offered with both hands." Sadly, Timothy refused at this time, but he was later taken in by a local social worker instead.

On June 15th we headed to the rehab in Manila again for the monthly visit. We took Mark and Matthew with us. Both boys had remained off solvents, with Mark in school and Matthew working. We knew it would be a nice surprise for the rehab boys to see them. We also took Simon with us because he wanted to see his friends. We wanted him to see what the conditions at the rehab were like in the hope that he would make a definite decision not to end up there. The visit went well, with all of the rehab boys talking to Mark and Matthew.

Peter, also from Olongapo, burst into tears when he saw Matthew, so Matthew had to spend a lot of time comforting him. Peter had been at the centre for a long time with no visitors and had recognised Matthew from the street. We welcomed all of the boys from Olongapo into our group every month. The staff and other boys referred to us as the "Olongapo group" and arranged a large table for us to provide food and to spend time chatting with the boys. I wished there was a group like this for every city or area as it was something for the boys to look forward to every month. Our large group became like a family gathering.

We celebrated Joel's birthday, having brought him a big cake. I didn't tell the others that, on the bridge, Joel had once told me that his birthday was in October and demanded that I give him a present. When I had refused, he got really upset and angry, so I gave him some jumping balls that I had in my bag as a gift and said, "Happy

Birthday." He had accepted the gift quietly, but the truth was exposed when we discovered his actual birthday and I understood his subdued response, as it hadn't been his birthday at all. But, I saw that Joel was changing. He said that he wanted to live with the family after rehab, and they agreed.

We gave the boys proper sleeping mats that we had purchased. I wanted to buy mats for all of the children, but I needed some time to work out the details. I asked the social workers and told the family that I would get the money together if they could find something suitable. It was arranged and, during the visit in August, the sleeping mats were given for all of the children at the centre. The main purpose was to try and prevent the recurrence of scabies and allow the children to have a decent rest. They got up at 5 am to start exercises and always looked exhausted whenever we visited them.

Again, it was hard to leave, but the boys were so used to seeing me turning up unexpectedly that they didn't believe it when I said I definitely wouldn't be back until the following year. When leaving, we told Simon he had to stay there, as a joke, and he looked horrified. We asked him whether he wanted to end up as a resident and he said no and that it was a horrible place. However, in the van on the way back, he became restless and said he was going to run away back to the street again. I couldn't believe it, after what he had just seen. I really couldn't understand what was going on with him and thought maybe it was related to an actual addiction to the solvents, as it seemed the only explanation. I worried about him as I knew that he was undecided. A short while after the family got back, he ran back to the street again.

Back in Olongapo, I determined to locate Simon, who wasn't taking his medicine, and Reuben who had also run away from the family. I found Simon with another boy high on solvents, they were playing pogs in the street. They had a small boy, about three years old, with them and they were supervising the child, who was the brother of Simon's friend. I scolded them that they were in no fit state to be looking after the younger child. Simon told me he would go back to the family "tomorrow." The boys said this frequently, but we learned to interpret it as their intention never to go home. We learned that, if we wanted to make progress, we had to get them to do things then and there, otherwise it wouldn't happen. In the end, I had to leave Simon on the street, but I was so upset by his state of health that I couldn't sleep.

Another day, I found Reuben very dirty and sad, so I took him and his friends for food at a local restaurant as a peace offering. When I first saw him, he walked the other way and refused to talk to me. I went after him and said sorry for whatever I had done, and I told him I would buy him food. At first, he refused because he was stubborn, but when I started walking away with his friends, he joined us. One of the other boys, Samuel, I knew already. Samuel told me that Reuben was living at his house, which seemed like a good idea rather than him being on the street. I went to visit Samuel's family with the two boys to check out the situation and found that the boys were sleeping in a really small room at the top of a ladder. There wasn't much ventilation so it was hot, but at least Reuben was off the street, so I told him it was okay. I sat and talked with Samuel's family for a while. There were many children and neither of the parents had work. Later, I arranged to replace a faulty light bulb so the boys could see upstairs, and I told the family that I would bring them a Bible.

I returned on another day with the promised Bible and saw Reuben knocking a tree with a wooden stick to try and get the fruit on it to fall on the ground. He was very subdued. I gave Samuel's family the Bible and prayed with them. But they told me that Samuel refused to attend school and they were worried about Reuben's influence on him. I supported Reuben staying there, as I didn't want to see him back on the street. But, I knew that he had moved around from one house to another over the years and always ended up back on the street, which he described as his "home." When I left, the boys convinced me to buy them flip flops because Samuel's were broken. Reuben promised that he wouldn't sell then but later broke his promise and then left the house for the street once again.

On our last day in Olongapo, I saw Reuben high on solvents, alone, and miserable outside a pub. He refused to speak to me still, and I was sad. I spent twenty minutes trying to persuade him to leave the street, and telling him that he would end up in rehab otherwise, but he just ignored me. I told him then that I would report him and the other boys left on the street to DSWD. I had no choice, as I couldn't stand to watch them destroy their lives. I hated to do it, as I knew it could damage the relationships I had built up with the boys if I reported their locations to their "enemy", but I felt I had no alternative. I asked the family to inform DSWD about the boys before I left Olongapo.

CHAPTER THIRTY-TWO

Miles Apart

When the boys were taken from the street by DSWD staff, the first place they were taken to was the Centre for Youth in Olongapo. This is a government facility used to hold the boys, pending their transfer to rehab or back to their families. It isn't really suitable for long-term care, due to the lack of available resources. However, the centre had been completely refurbished by a foreign charity, making it possible for up to twenty boys to live there. There were staff on duty twenty-four-seven and social workers were present during the day. The charity also provided funding for days out and some other activities.

Although there was room for improvement, as the boys didn't have a full programme, it was a lot better than them being on the street or in rehab. The centre was also working on getting the children enrolled in local schools. The general rule was that the younger boys and those who were well behaved and who didn't run away remained at the centre. Those who were addicted to solvents or who tried to escape would have their court papers processed for rehab in Manila.

Soon after the ship left Subic Bay for the last time, Simon and Reuben were caught by the DSWD staff and taken to the Centre for Youth. The Christian family visited them, but in the photos, the boys looked hopeless—all the life had gone from their faces. Reuben who had been officially registered as the family's foster son begged them to take him home. But, they had already decided that he needed to stay somewhere else as he kept running away. I continued funding Simon's medical treatment whilst he stayed at the centre.

In the end, both boys ran away from the centre and by the time they were recaptured, a court order had been processed for Simon to go to rehab. His rehab spell was agreed on the basis that I would continue to fund his medical care whilst he was there. I didn't really see an alternative because we had tried everything else. I couldn't believe Simon had been so foolish. He had seen what the rehab was like but had still chosen to throw away a year of his life. Reuben was kept at the centre for some time because he was afraid of going to rehab, and he had seemed to be settling down. But eventually he ran away several times and the DSWD obtained a court order for him to go to rehab too.

The family continued to visit the boys as I finished my commitment on Logos Hope, and I received regular reports about what was going on. The group of people heading to rehab for the monthly visit grew larger as family members of the boys accompanied the family. Simon had an emotional reunion with his father and sister during one of the visits. Other boys were taken to rehab using our "taxi service," and the family took some boys from the rehab back to Olongapo on their release. I felt it was beneficial because the family were giving spiritual input to the boys and their families and maintaining the relationships with the boys during their captivity.

I received the following message, from the boys in rehab, initiated by Paul, on September 5th, 2013 which was my birthday.

"Dear Natalie, How are you? I hope you are fine wherever you are. Always take care and bear in mind that we love you. Thank you for taking care of us when we were still outside and it is because of you that we are out of drugs, also the family. Because of you, we came to get close to GOD. I hope, after our time here in the place of recovery, we could be together. I promise I will never go away again and I will never sleep in church. I will always listen to your advice."

This confirmed the family's observations that Paul was taking his faith seriously in the rehab. I was also given a beautiful swan made from coloured paper with my name forming part of the design, which had been made by Paul and the other boys. The rehab staff were trying to find ways for the boys to earn a bit of money, so they taught them origami. The gifts were really very good, but unfortunately, the advertising and maybe the market weren't, so the project didn't really take off.

CHAPTER THIRTY-THREE

Olongapo Christian Help and Hope

The decision to return to the Philippines after my commitment on board Logos Hope had already been made. The question remained, where in the Philippines? I had been to Cebu, Manila, San Fernando, Puerto Princesa, and, of course, Olongapo. I had received offers of work from some of the places, but mostly in orphanages. People hear, "she works with street children" and they immediately think "orphanage" not "evangelist."

I obviously formed strong bonds with the street teenagers on the bridge. And over time, I came to love and care for them not just as street children but as if they were my own children. I would've done anything to see them leave the street and the drugs. But, the ultimate goal was always to see their lives totally changed by the transformation that could only come through Jesus and the hope that is found in Him. I didn't want to make the children dependent on me or anyone else. God loved the children much more than I could have done and He understood exactly what was going on in their lives and why they made the decisions they did. He was the only one who could truly help them.

At times, the poverty and need had been so overwhelming, and the situations so desperate, that practical help had become the priority for that time. But it remained true that a person could be given all of the food and material help in the world, but if they died without Jesus, they would spend an eternity in hell. After my time on the ship, my slogan became "Help and hope must go hand in hand."

Leaving the Logos Hope after two years was a struggle for most people. However, I can honestly say that it wasn't for me. I had found the final few months on-board very hard as I waited to finish my commitment so that I could return to the Philippines independently. As our van left the ship, to head for the airport in the middle of the night in September 2013, I boldly shouted "Freedom!" causing everyone to laugh. Unfortunately, ten minutes later, we had to return to the ship after being pulled over by the police for making a wrong turn and then realising that someone had left their laptop behind. Needless to say, the others blamed me for my premature jubilation!

Having said this, I learnt a lot of things on the ship which are documented in my book *The Logos Life*. I am grateful to God for my experiences and the many ministry opportunities, and especially for the future path that was mapped out for me during my time on-board. This had been a major prayer request on heading to the ship in 2011.

Due to my relatively short time back in the UK, I don't think re-entry really hit me as it did some other crew members who had difficulties for months afterwards.

Knowing that I would be returning to the Philippines longer-term, I set up a small charity, *Olongapo Christian Help and Hope*. In layman terms, the purposes were: to "Spread the Gospel of Jesus" and to "Help the poor." The official purposes were:

- *To advance the Christian religion in Olongapo, Philippines and the surrounding areas for the benefit of the public, through distributing literature and verbally sharing to enlighten others about the Christian religion.*
- *The prevention or relief of poverty in Olongapo, Philippines and the surrounding areas by providing: sponsorship, grants, items, and ser-vices to individuals and families in need.*
- *The relief of financial hardship among people living or working in Olongapo, Philippines and the surrounding areas by providing such persons with goods/services which they could not otherwise afford through lack of means.*

Once the charity was established, I put my affairs in order and sold nearly everything that I owned on Ebay, which was a challenge as I had been living in a three-bedroomed house. I ended up with just four boxes of personal effects! Then I prepared for a longer term return to the Philippines. After a few weeks in England, I was desperate to get back to the ministry with the boys and away from the cold weather! I finally booked my flight and after fifteen and a half hours arrived in Manila on 12th December 2013 less than two months after I had landed back in England after leaving the ship!

CHAPTER THIRTY-FOUR

Centre for Youth

One of the first things I did when I arrived back in the Philippines was to visit the Centre for Youth to get to know the DSWD staff there. I had heard a lot about the centre from the Christian family and I wanted to see if any of my boys were still living there. When I first arrived, the social worker was quite cool with me. After I had been talking about the purpose of my visit for a while she suddenly said, "What did you say your name was?" and I said "Natalie." She smiled and said, "Oh so you're Miss Natalie!"

A lot of the boys had been talking about me, but as I only really knew the "rugby boys," who tended to be the naughtier ones, most of them had run away or were in rehab. I was pleased that the boys had been saying positive things about me after some of the negative things that they had said to me before I had left. It proved that they didn't really mean the harsh things they had said in the heat of the moment. I believed that they would always be happy to see me if I found a way to visit them wherever they were.

After establishing my identity, the social workers were very friendly and helpful and shared information if it would help the boys. Prior to that, my attitude towards DSWD had been largely shaped by stories from the boys, as this was my only source of information. However, the Christian family had a good relationship with DSWD and, after leaving the ship, I had started to see things differently as I heard about some of the good things that were being done.

On meeting the social workers personally, I was amazed by their levels of knowledge about the individual boys that I had been working with. They had many years of experience in dealing with the families of the boys. It was useful for all of us to talk as we were able to fill in the gaps for each other. For example, they told me that in 2012 they had obtained court orders for Solomon and Luke to go to rehab. They hadn't been able to locate the boys and so had been forced to cancel the orders. I told them that, during our ministry, Solomon had gone home and back to school and that Luke's family had moved to Manila. In turn, they were able to give me information about the family backgrounds of the boys which really helped me to better understand their behaviour. I could then discern whether I should be persuading them to go back home, to the youth centre or to rehab!

My first invitation to see the boys at the Centre for Youth was to attend their Christmas party. At this time, I only recognised one boy, Malachi. Unfortunately, Malachi kept running away from the centre and eventually, he was processed for rehab despite being only nine years old.

On another occasion, Isaac had been captured. He looked miserable and was pretty non-communicative. He had been one of the tougher boys on the street, but at least he acknowledged me. He asked me to bring some biscuits the next time I visited. I was surprised by the request, small things seemed to assume great importance in the lives of the boys. There were already papers for Isaac to go to rehab. During a further visit, a week later, another familiar face, Solomon. He approached me saying, "Ma'am Natalie, it's me, Solomon," as if he was afraid I wouldn't recognise him. I acknowledged him, and then he sat down in a heap looking miserable. I was especially sad to see him because I had thought he had returned to school permanently. Both of the boys were due to be transferred to rehab because they wouldn't settle down at the Centre for Youth. Solomon even tried to saw the bars off the window during the night in an attempt to escape!

At the centre, I joined a Christian programme with a local church. We taught the boys the story of the lost son and the lost sheep from the Bible. For the lost son, we played a game, parts of the story were placed on pieces of paper inside balloons and the boys had to burst them to construct the story. For the lost sheep, the boys wrote their names and ages on an individual paper sheep. The game involved moving around the room to music and, when the music stopped, we picked a sheep and called out the name. All of the boys had to gather round and hug the boy whose name had been called. We abandoned the game when, perhaps predictably, it descended into chaos as the boys shoved and squashed each other. Later, I hid all of the sheep outside for the boys to find. Isaac became very excited when he found the sheep with his name on it stuck to the underside of a table. He shouted enthusiastically, "Hey look! I've found my sheep!" His response mirrored the shepherd's in the parable which was an unexpected bonus for those who had been teaching the story.

I shared the *Wordless Book* with the boys. There is a fuller explanation at the end of this book, but in brief, it is a book of different coloured papers. The first is yellow and represents heaven, then black for sin, red for Jesus' blood, white for a clean and new life with sins forgiven, and green for growth. It is a really simple way to share the Gospel that I learnt on-board Logos Hope. I used it a lot especially when sharing with children. I avoided my usual error of asking the boys what made them grow. Of course, they answered "food" which tended to put an end to any meaningful lessons. I had learned instead to ask, "What makes you grow closer to God?" Afterwards, the boys keenly stood and jostled each other in an impatient line as I painted the colours of the *Wordless Book* on their arms, to help them remember the Gospel.

My newly formed charity donated Christian books and Bibles in the local language to the Centre for Youth and to some other local institutions. The staff were instructed to distribute Bibles to those leaving the centre and informed that they would be replaced. It was really important for them to have access to good quality Christian literature in their own language—the few books already in their library were in English which most of the boys couldn't read.

CHAPTER THIRTY-FIVE

Reunited

On 14th December 2013, I joined the family for their pre-Christmas rehab visit. It was an event to remember. We hired two vans, due to the numbers of family members and other people wanting to join the visit. We also prepared food and gifts for a special celebration. It would be a surprise for the boys. I had previously told them I wouldn't visit again until the following year. They had no idea I had finished my ship commitment and returned to Olongapo.

At that time, I met Joel's father, step-mother and one of his step-sisters, Simon's dad and sister, Paul's grandma and some other relatives that accompanied us from Olongapo. It was a really great day. A highlight was Joel's emotional reunion with his father and watching him playing with his step-sister. We had had to persuade Joel to allow his father to join the visit as they had been estranged. He agreed, on the basis that, if he told us where his family were living, we wouldn't make him go back and live with them again in the future. We accepted his condition in the hope that Joel and his father would rebuild their relationship and Joel would later change his mind.

A couple of things overshadowed the celebration. Adam burst into tears and wouldn't stop crying when he saw that there was no one to visit him. I was surprised because I hadn't realised how the lack of visitors was affecting him. He had never mentioned it and I rarely saw him show any emotion. All of our attempts to console him failed so I determined that we must bring him a visitor on our subsequent visit.

Paul sat with his grandma, but there was little warmth between them and they weren't really communicating properly. A rehab social worker had private family discussions with all of the relatives and the boys. It was finally established that Paul's grandma wasn't actually his grandma, she had just been a neighbour of his mother. She was in her sixties and didn't want the responsibility of looking after Paul on his release. She didn't want to continue to visit him. Apparently, Paul's mother had given him to her when he was a baby and said, "Here, this is your son now." We were unable to establish whether her story was true because she didn't visit Paul again. We wondered whether she was just seeking to transfer responsibility due to a lack of funding, a lack of interest or an inability to carry the burden.

There were ongoing discussions concerning where the boys would live when they left rehab. Joel and Paul wanted to live with the Christian family, Adam wasn't really sure, and Simon wanted to return to live with his father and sister. It was possible for any of the boys to live at the Centre for Youth, but where there were suitable family members that was obviously preferable.

During the visit, the social worker informed us that she had applied to the court for Simon to be immediately released because they couldn't deal with his heart condition in the rehab. My charity continued to fund his regular hospital check-ups and daily medication. I was worried that in comparison to the other boys, he wasn't being effectively rehabilitated. He didn't have to participate in the exercise programs and other activities due to his health problems. The other boys said that he was having an easy ride. However, the prospect of his early release after just a few months was even more of a concern. I could tell that his attitude hadn't changed and, despite his health concerns, he would be likely to go straight back to the street and the solvents. I hoped and prayed that the release order would be delayed until a suitable alternative could be found for Simon.

On 4th January 2014, we again visited the rehab, but without Joel's father who had agreed to accompany us. He had been drinking, which was a disappointment. We had located Adam's stepfather a few weeks before the visit and had arranged to pick him up, but he hadn't arrived at the meeting point. I refused to go to the rehab without him as images of Adam's distress during our previous visit played on my mind. Two of us left the others waiting in the van and went to his house which seemed to be in the middle of nowhere. It was a wooden shack in the middle of an open area but there was nobody at home. Discouraged, we turned to leave but found ourselves face to face with Adam's stepfather. I recognised him from photos the family had taken when they had arranged the pick-up. He was with two young children. Elated, I reminded him of the visit expecting that he would apologise and immediately accompany us. Instead, he pointed to what appeared to be an old pile of bricks and said that he had to guard it on behalf of his neighbour, apparently it was a house! Realising it was just an excuse, but taking control of the situation, I asked a neighbour whether he could instead guard the brick pile. He agreed but Adam's stepfather still refused to accompany us.

I became quite animated. I told him how upset Adam had been during our previous visit and that we must take him a visitor. At this point, he said he wasn't even related to Adam—his relatives lived somewhere else and didn't want anything to do with him. I was really fed up of hearing excuses from one parent after another. I ended up practically begging the man to join us, to no avail. As a last resort, we suggested that one of the children, who were Adam's half-siblings, might be sufficient. This seemed better than nothing and thankfully, the boy, who was aged about ten, willingly agreed.

The man then added insult to injury by informing us that he didn't want Adam returning to live with him after rehab. He said that he was afraid of him and what he might do. Adam had told us previously that he had been badly beaten by his step-father which was one of the reasons he had run away in the first place.

When we arrived at the rehab, Adam was pleased to see his half-sibling. But, unfortunately, somebody told him what had happened and how I had tried to persuade his "step-father" to visit. I had wanted to keep it a secret, in case it would hurt him. I was worried because of his extreme emotion during the previous visit, but there was no visible reaction which was a relief.

The boys were beginning to struggle in the rehab and starting to misbehave. Paul was depressed due to the monotony and the others were desperate to get out. It had been especially hard over Christmas, due to having had no visitors which reminded them of their loneliness. They commented that our previous visit had also been short, due to traffic delays. It was a hard visit because the boys were subdued, but we tried to make the best of it.

My plan to encourage local churches to join our ministry in the rehab surfaced again. I mapped the churches nearby. The name of one of the nearest churches rang a bell. The pastor from Olongapo that had met the boys on the bridge had moved to the church near the rehab! I knew the pastor quite well and he definitely had a heart for the boys. I contacted him to ask whether his new church might consider a regular visiting schedule at the centre. The rehab staff were very keen on the idea, some of them were Christians. The pastor was enthusiastic about the opportunity and suggested that some of his members might join us for a visit so that they could meet the staff. I was elated thinking that God was orchestrating things. I looked forward to the meeting and tying things up.

At around that time, for a number of reasons, the Christian family decided that they didn't want the boys returning to live with them after rehab. The family wanted to focus on their own ministry and for their older foster boys to find work outside the home. They were concerned that the boys would get in trouble if there was no-one at the house to supervise them. I agreed with their observation but knew it would be a blow for the boys who had been looking forward to living with the family.

I was worried about taking over the coordination and organisation of the monthly visits to the rehab without the support of the family. Money wasn't a big issue, but, rounding up relatives, preparing food, buying medicine and doing everything else on my own would be a huge task especially with my limited language ability. The family helpfully agreed to continue to be involved with the preparations for the February visit. I was grateful as it allowed me some time to make decisions about the longer-term future of the ministry.

During this visit, I would need to break the news to the boys. The timing wasn't great because it was so close to them being released.

When we arrived, we found that Paul and Simon were on restriction. Paul, for being rude to one of the guards, and Simon for fighting. Paul had been rude because he was bored and hadn't wanted to exercise that day. I reprimanded him reminding that he must behave himself. He might otherwise be punished by being kept longer in rehab. Adam, who tended to get into trouble for fighting, was doing well with good reports.

I reassured Paul that in the absence of the family I would still be there for him, he took the news well. He requested that I try and find him a Christian foster family because he was worried about returning to the Centre for Youth due to the influences and pressures of former friends. I couldn't promise anything as I knew this would be a tough task but I said I would do my best.

On hearing the news, Joel promptly burst into tears. He was just so disappointed, having pinned all of his hopes on going back to the family. However, I knew it would pass as he had only lived with them for two days. Deep down, I was hoping that he would return to his own family at some stage, maybe with financial support. Adam didn't seem bothered by the change in circumstance and said that he was happy to go back to the Centre for Youth.

The rehab social worker and I spoke to Joel's father alone. I mentioned that it had been brought to our attention that he hadn't accompanied us on our previous visit due to being drunk. We really wanted him to take responsibility for Joel and were concerned that he didn't seem to be taking responsibility even for himself. I worded my observations carefully thinking he might react aggressively, but he listened to everything I had to say. He responded that he found the influence of his friends and the temptations they placed in his path difficult to resist. I reminded him that he was an adult with a young wife and three small children in addition to Joel. He must find a way to deal with his friends and vices. I told him that Joel felt afraid of him due to abuses in the past. He admitted having been careless and not the father he should have been.

I shared my personal testimony—I knew the only answer to his desperation was found in Jesus. I shared how I also had been hopeless and lost in a world of drink and other vices, and how Jesus had changed my life. The social worker asked how he felt about my story, and he said he was overwhelmed by what he had heard. I could see he needed some time to reflect.

In the van on the way back to Olongapo, thinking it might be the last opportunity, I gave all of the boys' relatives Bibles and invited them to church the following day.

CHAPTER THIRTY-SIX

Rugby Boys in Church

The following morning, when I arrived at the church, the pastor said that someone had stopped by to ask if it was "Natalie's church." On receiving confirmation, he had returned to get his whole family. After a few minutes, Joel's dad, step-mum, and the three small children walked into the church. It was a moving moment when they all traipsed in because I hadn't really thought they would take me up on the invitation.

They attended several times after that initial step. Simon's dad and sister also turned up a few times. I prayed that they would not just attend the church but would come under conviction of sin when hearing the Gospel. I was encouraged by their willingness to make the effort to be there.

I also invited the older boys that I knew from the street to accompany me to church. During a heart to heart with James, the boy who kept getting a job and then losing it in an earlier chapter, I invited him to go to church with me on the following Sunday. I pointed out that a new start was the only way to really change his life. To my surprise, he agreed and told me to collect him at a designated meeting place. I turned up but there was no one there. His brother, working in the area, informed me that he was asleep in a jeepney nearby. I knew that I would probably have to round the boys up to get them to actually go to church—they tended to make decisions on the spur of the moment, they didn't plan ahead.

I approached the jeepney and saw that there were some boys asleep in the back of it stretched out across the seats. There were a lot of older men hanging around chatting. I could see three boys sleeping: James, Caleb, who was twelve, and a boy I didn't know. I had met Caleb for the first time a few weeks before finding him asleep in the jeepney. I had heard that he had been released from rehab and, within a few weeks, was back on the street abusing solvents. There was already another court order for him to be returned to rehab. It was all such a waste. I had tried to convince him that he should talk to the social workers, maybe they would cancel the order. He said he would "tomorrow" and I knew he would just end up back in rehab.

I woke the boys up and told them to get up because we were going to church in a voice that said, "Don't argue with me." The older males standing by ceased their chatter and looked shocked. A white foreign female had just instructed a load of street boys that they were going to church! The boys obediently got up and started wiping their faces and looking confused. They followed me to McDonald's for breakfast as I knew they wouldn't concentrate at all if they were hungry. Then we got straight into a jeepney and headed to church. On the way, I accidentally walked into the roof of a house, banging my head, which the boys thought was highly amusing, especially as I had been concerned about a bruise on Caleb's head.

They boys looked a bit out of place in the church, but people welcomed them and asked for their names. The church members even gave them new T-shirts to replace their dirty, holey ones. They were a bit subdued at first, probably wondering how they had ended up there, as it had all happened while they were still half asleep. They came to life when the pastor asked people if they had anything they wanted to thank God for. The boys then started poking me and telling me to stand up and share my blessing, which I refused to do. Shortly after that, and during the sermon which was in English, they all fell asleep.

After the service, I gave James his own personal New Testament which he was happy to receive. He asked if we could visit one of his friends in the police cells as we walked past the station. I agreed wondering what I would say as there had been no time to prepare. On being granted permission to talk to the prisoners, we found that there were eight men in one cell which was only about three metres square.

James was proudly carrying his new Bible, but the prisoners caught sight of it and of course, they all wanted one too. I promised to return on a future date with more Bibles, but they protested. They claimed they were being transferred out of the local police cell and into the main prison the following day. Not often finding myself in a position where people were begging me for Bibles, I agreed to go and get some immediately. The guards agreed to a revisit later in the day, but there was a condition, they wanted Bibles too! Therefore, I ended up giving everyone in the station New Testaments, including a lady who was making a complaint in the station who demanded her copy on my return.

James and I then went to the Centre for Youth with some young people from my church. We had planned a social activity for the church youth to meet the street youth. The "rugby boys" at the centre, especially Solomon and Isaac, were excited to see James, whom they knew from the street as one of their leaders. However, the church youth were shocked by some of the language used by the street youth. Even more so, when during a friendly game of basketball, one of the street youth challenged one of the church youth to a fight over a misdirected throw!

James later asked me if I would like to visit his family home. I asked some church members to accompany us. I was keen to meet his family and somewhat curious—it was rare to receive an invite and I often didn't know much about the family backgrounds of the boys. We walked up a steep concrete staircase in the dark for what seemed like over a hundred steps. On reaching the top, we were immediately confronted by a teenage girl who turned out to be James' sister. Apparently, it was her birthday and they were in the middle of the celebration. On seeing James, she obviously faced a variety of mixed emotions as she screamed with delight and hugged him, then punched him in anger, and then burst into tears.

I was surprised to see that James' family lived in a really nice house, although it was shared by a lot of people. James' father had died, but his mother held a good job. She was in a position of influence that would easily allow her to find James a good job if he would allow her to. But James and his brothers had rejected the help as they wanted to make it on their own, so to speak. I had to respect their decision although it hadn't worked out that well—they were all on the street taking solvents.

James agreed to remain at the house with his family. He was still living there several months later although he hadn't turned up to church on the following Sunday having said he would. I had by that point learned the three "P's" to avoid discouragement: patience, persistence and prayer. I prayed that James wouldn't lapse back into his old ways and that he would read the New Testament that I had given him.

CHAPTER THIRTY-SEVEN

My Wake Up Call

In February 2014, after a brief visit to England, I returned to Olongapo with my close friend Penny, who was to visit for two weeks. I had rented an apartment in New Cabalan (forty-five minute jeepney ride from the bridge) and rarely visited the original bridge ministry area as the boys had moved on. The smaller groups that were left on the street continued to abuse solvents under other bridges but they were relatively discreet places. I asked the police and DSWD a few times where the "rugby boys" had moved to, but no one seemed to know. I hoped, rather than believed, that their absence meant that they had all stopped the solvent abuse. I knew there would always be some that continued.

One early evening, Penny and I were walking across a bridge in an unfamiliar part of the city looking for somewhere to eat. Suddenly, out of the corner of my eye, I saw a dirty and partially clothed figure next to the barrier that led down under the bridge. The figure rushed to a green wheelie bin, pulled the lid open, rummaged around for a few seconds, and scurried away again. It all happened so quickly that, although I had seen the boy, I hadn't really noticed or paid much attention so we carried on walking along the road. It was Penny who said, "Maybe he is one of them?" I knew she meant a "rugby boy." It crossed my mind that the timing of the encounter was a little inconvenient. I was a bit worried about talking to the boy and getting Penny involved. It was one thing to put myself in this type of situation. However, Penny seemed just as keen as I was to investigate further.

It was often at times when I was busy with something else that I saw the boys. But it was usually possible to quickly rearrange my priorities. After all, what was more important than starting a conversation that might change, or even save, a person's life? There may not have been another opportunity for that person to hear about the hope that can only be found in Jesus. To hear that there was any type of hope was often amazing news to these invisible children. They had abandoned the hope that they had been clinging onto many years before.

It was almost always time that was required to take the first crucial step in reaching out to a lost person. Buying food was often necessary as a tool to open the door to share with them and to demonstrate God's love in action, but it was not the most important factor. Christians should help practically when possible as per James 2 vs 16,

"If you say to your brother, 'Go, I wish you well, stay warm and well fed,' but do nothing about his physical needs, what good is this?"

Sometimes I found it difficult to strike the right balance between help and hope when building new relationships with the street boys and other homeless people. There were times when I really was committed with something important or with others who didn't share my concern for the boys and I was, therefore, unable to give them my time or attention. It was at these times that I felt pretty inadequate and frustrated. In January 2014, when I was on the way to Clark Airport in Angeles City, my attention was drawn to a large group of "rugby boys" and girls. Having initially walked past thinking there was nothing I could do, I felt convicted and returned to talk to them. I did have to walk away after a short period of time—the area was a long way out of Olongapo and I had no contacts there. My heart wanted to move there for a few months to work with the boys on a daily basis. But I knew it was unrealistic and I had to trust that God was looking after the children. I prayed that a local church would take responsibility for ministering to them when the time was right.

On another occasion, I was rushing to get somewhere and a lady asked me for money to feed her children. Normally, I made it a practice never to give money. If the person had an addiction it could make things worse. However, I could see that the poor lady was just trying to provide for her family so I gave her a very small amount of money. Afterwards, I was convicted that I had given the money partly to get rid of the lady because my mind was on other things and I hadn't had time for her. I hadn't even told her the reason for the gift. The lady probably went away thinking that I was just a rich foreigner or a kind stranger. Either way, it had been useless spiritually. I thought about the lady a lot afterwards. I made a firm decision that whenever I gave anything I would always take the time to share the reason for the gift, even if it was hope in very basic terms, for example, "Jesus loves you and this is from Him."

There were also times on the ship when I had very little money and was unable to help practically. I had to learn to accept this and realise that I could not do everything. I became upset one day as I had stopped to talk to an older homeless lady. Afterwards, I felt totally useless as I hadn't been able to offer her what she really needed practically. I had encouraged her to seek God for her needs and to attend a local church. A friend reminded me that we should help practically when we were able but that we shouldn't allow the enemy to discourage us when it wasn't possible.

Returning to the figure that had emerged from under the bridge, Penny and I stopped and retraced our steps. I walked around the bridge barrier and down into the dark space underneath it, feeling a tiny bit afraid of what I might find. I moved forward gradually as my eyes adjusted to the darkness and, as I called out, two figures slowly and hesitantly moved towards me. The two boys were really filthy dirty and very thin, aged about fifteen or sixteen. I engaged them in basic conversation, establishing names and that they were living under the bridge.

I could see Penny watching from the bridge. She suggested we get some food, so we took them to Jollibee, a fast-food restaurant nearby, (the Filipino equivalent of McDonald's.) The local people watched with astonishment as we walked along the street with the boys. They smelt strongly of solvents and seemed a bit dazed and confused. One of the boys had visible traces of glue on his face and in his hair. He was so dirty and dishevelled that he looked almost animal-like, having lost the ability and motivation to care for himself or his appearance. I hadn't seen boys in that state before as my "bridge boys" were relatively clean and lucid in comparison.

We sat with the boys and chatted with them whilst they ate, which they did slowly. A side effect of the drugs was that they made the children feel full so that when they ate proper food they sometimes felt ill or couldn't eat much until their bodies re-adjusted. It is similar to the effect of not eating at all for a few days, the stomach shuts down and it's hard to start eating again. I told the boys about the dangers of the solvents and discovered that they knew some of my bridge boys. We shared the Gospel with them and invited them to attend a local church before leaving them to finish their meal.

Although I looked for them, I didn't see these boys again. I thought about them a lot and kept replaying what had happened in my mind. My only mental comparison was to some kind of animal scurrying around and rooting through rubbish. My mind hadn't even registered that they were humans. I could see how easy it was for the boys to become invisible to locals, especially when the sight of them high on drugs and searching through rubbish bins became normal, and blended in with everything else that was happening. I realised with shock that *I* hadn't really seen the boys. They had become invisible to me, as well as the many other people milling around. I determined and hoped that I would keep my eyes open in the future and not allow this to happen again.

CHAPTER THIRTY-EIGHT

Grading Celebration Day

The time arrived for me to visit the rehab again, as although I had decided not to continue the monthly van run, I had made a promise that I would visit the boys once a month. I planned to visit using public transport, but I felt guilty as I knew that some family members really wanted to see their children, particularly Simon's dad and sister, who had been faithful in their monthly attendance. I knew that they couldn't afford to visit by themselves and that Simon's dad might find it difficult on public transport due to his disability.

In the end, I spoke to a social worker at the Centre for Youth about the situation, she suggested we use one of their vans and drivers to save money. My charity could cover the fuel, food, and anything else required. She also wanted to accompany us, as she hadn't visited the boys at the rehab for a long time and she was responsible for them. Additionally, the rehab staff had planned a special celebration for the boy's completion of their school year grade, and we were invited.

On 14th March 2014, we attended the celebration at the rehab in Manila. Simon's father and sister were the only relatives that accompanied us. I was a bit disappointed that Joel's family hadn't made the effort as they had been given advance notice. The pastor from the local church who wanted to begin ministry in the centre, also joined us on that day, with five ladies from his church. It was a real encouragement as they met some of the boys and the staff. They were hoping to begin a formal children's programme at the rehab.

The rehab boys looked smart in their white T-shirts and trousers, prepared specially for the occasion. I was pleased that they seemed to be in better spirits than the previous visit and were looking forward to their imminent release. The celebration began just after we arrived, and then continued for hours with long speeches from various important looking officials. The boys looked pretty bored and repeatedly attempted to join us at the tables nearby where we were waiting to eat the food we had brought for them. Every time they thought the speeches had finished someone else stood up to speak and they were forced to traipse dejectedly back to their seats.

For the main event, the boys' names were called out one at a time and they walked in single file onto the stage to be presented with their certificates. Adam completed Kindergarten, Simon and Joel, grade two and three, and Paul grade four. Afterwards, there were special awards for leadership and good behaviour. Several of our boys received medals, including Paul, who asked me to stand on stage with him as his petitioner. I was honoured, but some of the other boys in the audience thought it was funny because I obviously wasn't his parent. There was an audible undercurrent of sniggering as we walked together to the stage. I felt slightly uncomfortable for Paul's sake, but he didn't seem bothered and just ignored them, collected his medal, had his photo taken and that was that.

Later, as we were eating, Joel requested permission for Isaac and Solomon to join us. In the hype and activity, I had forgotten that they had already been transferred to the centre from Olongapo just a week earlier. I immediately asked the social worker if they could join us because we had brought food for them. After ten minutes the two boys appeared, their heads having been shaved. I was shocked to see them so physically altered from the lively, naughty boys that had been rushing around the Centre for Youth trying to escape only a week before. They looked small, afraid, dazed, and confused as if the life had been sucked out of them. I nearly cried when I saw them. They cheered up a little when they saw the big group of us waiting for them, and when I gave them a canteen slip with some money deposited.

After we had finished eating, I was sitting next to Isaac, the youngest of our boys at rehab, who looked really sad. He said something to me in Tagalog and the social worker translated, "Ma'am

Natalie when I can come back to Olongapo, I want to come and live with you at your house." The social worker told him that he would have to stay at the centre for a year and he burst into tears. I tried to comfort him without crying myself. Isaac had been one of the toughest boys when he was on the street, but reality had set in for him straight away. What he was really saying was, "Ma'am Natalie. Please give me another chance to do the right thing and take me away from this horrible place."

Unfortunately, I had no control over his detention as there were court orders for all of the boys to be in rehab. However, I promised to visit him every month and encouraged him to pray when he felt alone or to talk to the Christian social workers. He continued crying broken-heartedly for a while as he adjusted to the new information about his detention. Then it was time for us to leave so he turned and gave me a big hug.

As we were leaving, a social worker asked for my details because the director of the rehab had asked who I was as he had seen me with the boys and on the stage with Paul. The social worker had told him about the work we had been doing and that my charity was responsible for donating the sleeping mats for the boys. The director wanted to give some formal recognition of the help I had given them. I jokingly advised the social worker that, rather than recognising me, I would prefer it if he made sure the boys didn't have scabies on my next visit. Then, thinking that might not be the best way to make friends and influence people and wanting to preserve my good relationship with the rehab staff, I quickly withdrew my comment and gave my full name but requested no formal recognition. I couldn't think of anything worse than being hauled on stage and "recognised," but I knew that it was a big part of Filipino culture and I didn't want to offend anyone unnecessarily!

On this day, my emotions got the better of me as I walked out through the main gate. I had been suppressing them whilst inside in an effort not to upset the boys. It was just so hard to leave the new boys there, knowing that they would go through the same experience as our other boys had over the twelve-month period. I reminded myself that the others had looked and behaved in the same way when they had first been at the rehab. Over time they had really matured and developed into responsible young men due to the enforced discipline and strict regimes at the centre.

Conditions at the rehab were not great but the routines and daily devotions were good for the boys and helped to prepare them for life in the real world. They also receive a year of education. For some, it was their first year of schooling at the age of fifteen! Some of the staff were Christians and really cared for the children and no doubt prayed for them as well. It made a huge difference for these rejected children, who formed strong bonds with the social workers. It was just so hard to see them broken first, especially when they were just eleven or twelve. However, both Solomon and Isaac had had many chances in Olongapo, and I realised that rehab was the only way for them to learn their lesson and to stay off the street, and the solvents.

CHAPTER THIRTY-NINE

End of an Era

In March 2014, I began to believe that God was moving me on from Olongapo to another area of work in Manila. I started to finalise the ministry in Olongapo and made small attempts to help the families of the rehab boys prepare for the return of their children. I used charity funds to replace the roof on Simon's family's shack house, because it had been severely damaged in a flood, and I paid one month's worth of rent arrears for Joel's family.

It was then that I received a long awaited message from the Centre for Youth staff. Reuben had finally been located! I had spent many hours searching for him in the highways and byways since returning to Olongapo. I couldn't forget the ingrained memory of him alone, sad, and miserable when I had left on the previous occasion, and then the subsequent photos of his lifeless expression sent to me by the family. My searches were fruitless, and I thought that maybe he had gone to live elsewhere. Then I heard rumours of local sightings and started to hope that he might be found before I left.

Apart from having to go to the hospital for some tests, and feeling a bit under the weather, the staff said that he was okay and wanted to see me. As was the case with Joel, old hostilities were soon forgotten after even a small lapse of time. I visited him straight away and got half a hug, the other boys were there and he had to consider his image! Then I gave him a photo of us from the bridge days and I saw the appreciative smile before he managed to hide it as it wouldn't have been cool to be excited about something like this. He ate three of the apples and two of the oranges that I brought in quick succession, and then demanded that I buy him a music speaker! Things hadn't changed at all! I declined, not feeling the need to give him a reason but knowing that he would have no use for it in rehab as it would be confiscated. I was glad I wouldn't be there when they told him his intended destination, but I planned to visit him when he got there.

I visited the rehab alone in April, a big task as nine Olongapo boys appeared to see me and I had to try and communicate with them all with my still very basic Tagalog. This visit was especially difficult as the boys were hoping to leave, but I had no positive news for them as papers were still being processed. They were also hoping to see family members but the van run would need to be organised by someone else due to my move to Manila. I offered to continue funding the trip if DSWD wanted to co-ordinate it. The social worker was keen to continue but their vehicle had broken down with no definite date for repair so the plan had to be postponed.

After the visit charity funds paid for Paul to have a series of medical tests with a view to a potential transfer to a Christian children's home in Manila. He had expressed concern about returning to Olongapo and potentially succumbing to influences and vices from his past and I wanted to give him another option. I also received paperwork in relation to the transfer suggesting that Paul was two years older than I had originally believed. On the street, this wouldn't have been big news as the boys often lied about their ages. Paul had consistently told us that he was fourteen when we first met him, which meant that he was about to turn sixteen. However, the new information, (if true), made him about to turn eighteen instead! On discussion, it was clear that he hadn't known and definitely believed that he was fifteen turning sixteen. At my request, the social worker launched an investigation to determine the truth.

The transfer to the children's home didn't go ahead in the end for a number of reasons. The main one was that I felt Paul was going along with the decision to transfer on my advice rather than because he really wanted to. I was concerned about this as I didn't want to be responsible for making his life any more difficult than it already was. I was also worried that he wasn't ready to cut his ties with Olongapo.

He looked so sad at the prospect of being transferred alone and missing his friends that I decided it might not be wise.

We were all expecting Paul's medical test results to be negative, as although he had been diagnosed with TB, this had been over a year before and he had not experienced medical issues in rehab. Sadly, and surprisingly, he was diagnosed with hepatitis B for which there was no permanent cure. At around the same time, his release order came through from the court (the first one as the other boys had a different judge). Throughout the period, I dreaded receiving the result of our enquiry about Paul's age. I knew that potentially I would then have to inform him that in addition to having an incurable disease he had also lost two years of his life!

I visited the boys again towards the end of May 2014. I left the visit until later in the month hoping that I could join the social worker from Olongapo and that some of the boys would be able to be released. However, their vehicle was still broken in Olongapo so I visited alone again. On arrival, the boys were subdued and didn't seem interested in the Jollibee takeaway I had brought them, although they perked up after a while.

Simon was upset because his medical release order still hadn't come through from the judge. I was astounded because the release had originally been requested in November 2013, on the basis that the rehab didn't have sufficient resources to care for Simon adequately. It had been nearly eight months, which was the normal length of time for a child to stay in rehab. It seemed God had answered my original prayer for Simon to be effectively rehabilitated prior to his release.

Then, I discovered that Paul and another Olongapo boy had had a fight earlier in the day. The other boy had hit Paul on the head with a rock and Paul punched him in retaliation. Both boys were placed under "violation" and were not allowed to attend the visitation. I was advised that they were both crying in the dormitory.

Unfortunately, Isaac had a severe case of scabies (the worst I had seen) which was especially bad on his hands and feet which were covered in sores and bleeding so he could barely walk. I took him straight to the rehab clinic and paid for additional medicine but there was little else I could do and he seemed cheerful enough.

Other than that, the visit was pretty relaxed as the boys that were due for release knew that it would happen eventually and the new boys had settled down and were looking forward to starting school in June. Joel stated his earnest desire never to go back to the street or solvents and told me he was praying for me. The boys quoted Bible verses they had learnt in devotions and repeated the lyrics of Christian songs. I left them some Gospel tracts that I had with me and they immediately started reading them aloud. I was so encouraged by the discussions this day and by their obvious enthusiasm for Christian things. One older boy even told me that he had become a Christian in the rehab through a chaplain or staff member.

I had been preparing for the release of the first group of boys for a long time, having seen the journey begin. They were definitely ready to leave, and I was ready to help them get on with their lives in the real world. Looking back, it seemed like a lifetime had passed since I had first been to this place and seen those small, confused, fearful faces and had had to hold back the tears. The difference in the boys, both physically due to the absence of drugs, and in character due to the discipline was stark. I dared to hope that they had also been changed spiritually but ultimately this was the work of God and I had to leave it in His hands.

On this day in May, I once again walked out through the metal gated partition separating the rehab boys from the rest of the world. Then I headed up the hill towards the entrance gate. I turned and waved several times whilst walking up the hill and the boys reciprocated as they walked down the hill in the opposite direction back to their dormitory. I noticed a few boys looking back several times to see if I was still there, seeking their individual goodbyes. If they were feeling especially lonely or sad they would keep looking back until I had completely disappeared through the entrance gate. These were the times that I found it hard to leave them there. However, on this day, I was reminded that God would take care of them because

"In His hand is the life of every creature and the breath of all mankind." Job 12 vs 10.

Epilogue

When I arrived in Subic Bay in March 2012, I had no idea what was in store for me. If someone had told me in advance that I was to spend the following two years and beyond expending my best energies and emotions on the plight of a few street teenage boys, I would have laughed. If the same person had told me of the emotional ups and downs and frustrations I would have to go through in order to see just a little bit of change in just a few lives, maybe I would have reconsidered getting involved. But looking back, I can say that it was honestly worth it. A few lives changed drastically, and in others, there were small gradual changes over time. Each of the boys was precious to God and He desired that, *"None of them should be lost but that each of them should come to repentance."* 2 Peter 3 vs 9.

I learnt many lessons along the way, and after only a few years working with the boys, I am no expert. I made many mistakes, most of which have been documented, and a few of which have not! I hope that you might be able to think of ways to make a difference in the life of one or more of these "invisible" children. My biggest piece of advice is "start small," One of the smallest things we did which had the biggest impact was to learn the names of the boys and to use them. Whoever God calls you to help, I encourage you to treat them as individuals and to demonstrate that their lives are important. Constantly remind them that it is God who loves them and that this is the reason for your concern. Don't expect dramatic change straight away, but, be patient, persevere, and pray. Don't try and do everything, or you will end up doing nothing. Just do something. One person put it like this:

"I am only one, but still I am one. I cannot do everything, but still, I can do something; and because I cannot do everything, I will not refuse to do something that I can do." Helen Keller

In April 2014, I left Olongapo and moved to Cubao in Manila to begin working with a new church amongst the street homeless people and the "rugby boys." The motto of Christian Compassion Ministries, the charity of my church is *"How can we tell people about the love of Christ without showing them something of that love?"* This resonated with me and tied in perfectly with my charity's slogan *"Help and hope must go hand in hand."*

I knew that I would visit Olongapo from time to time because part of my heart remained there with the boys, at home with their families, at the Centre for Youth and with those still on the street. I had committed to being there for the boys if ever they needed help. I was determined to keep this promise, especially to the boys who had no one else, and to be a reliable and consistent figure in their lives as a constant reminder of God's love and care for them through His people.

In my experience, at the end of a true story like this, the reader is often left wondering what has happened to the people mentioned within. How did their lives turn out? Of course, only God knows their long-term future but *A Missionary in Manila* contains updates about several of the boys. You can read a little about the individual boys at the back of this book. You can also read about other aspects of my journey on-board Logos Hope in *The Logos Life.*

THE END

Please feel free to contact the author at natalie.vellacott@gmail.com. If you have enjoyed this book, the author would really appreciate it if you could leave a review Amazon and Goodreads. Thankyou!

The Individuals

Matthew (18)

Matthew was the main group leader that we spent a lot of time with as he appeared at the start of our ministry on the bridge. He had been on and off the street for many years. He had been to rehab at least twice and claims he became a Christian through a social worker during one of his rehab stints. He had massive problems with his family and couldn't live with them. As a result, he was a very angry man.

In 2017, Matthew was still working in Olongapo City at various low-paying jobs. Many of the older boys sold counterfeit DVD's in the city for just one hundred pesos a day and Matthew was often amongst them. Matthew claimed to have converted to Islam and even changed his name to reflect that. I haven't had contact with him for a long time but I believe he is still influencing the younger boys in a negative way.

Noah (9)

Noah was the youngest of our boys and the only one of our regulars attending school and not abusing solvents. He was in danger of becoming one of the next generation of "rugby boys" due to the amount of time he spent with them, but during our time on the bridge, he didn't succumb. His mother was working near to the bridge, hence the connection.

In 2014, Noah was still living with his mother in the general vicinity of the bridge and was still attending school. He was no longer hanging around with the group of boys as the group was disbanded during our work with the bridge boys. The last time I saw him, he was with his older brother and wearing his school uniform.

Rachel (16) and Jacob (17)

Rachel and Jacob appeared to be in a relationship. Initially, Jacob was always hanging around, sniffing solvents, begging, and making a nuisance of himself, but eventually he found a job and left the street. Rachel only appeared a few times on the bridge and was already holding a steady job.

I did not see Rachel or Jacob during my return visits to Olongapo City. I pray that they are still working and that Jacob has not returned to his former ways.

David (21)

David was another of the main group leaders and was good friends with Matthew. They had spent time in rehab together. David left the street early in our ministry, responding to his realisation that God loved him. He made a profession of faith and began attending a local Baptist church. He found a stable job and stayed well away from his former vices for over a year.

In 2014, David's friends reported that he was using solvents and drinking and that he was no longer attending the church. David advised me that he planned to attend the church on Easter Sunday and states that he is not back to his former ways. He is still working full time.

James (20)

James was another of our main group leaders but was less attached to the group. James appeared on the bridge at times but then left again. He was also abusing solvents. James obtained various low-paid jobs during our time with him, including selling food that he had cooked, but they were always short lived and he didn't seem able to hold a job for longer than a few weeks at a time.

James came to a church in Olongapo in 2014 and I was invited to his house and met his family. His dad had died a while ago. He seemed serious about changing his life, and his friends report that he has stayed at home and is not inhaling solvents.

Mark (16)

Mark was one of our biggest struggles. He claimed to be "born again" and had been attending church and Bible study but, after an incident involving a girl in July 2012, he dropped out of high school in his final year, began inhaling solvents, and living on the street. We began our ministry at around that time, not knowing that Mark was a newcomer. Mark had a mother, father, and brother, and his own room at the family home (unusual amongst the group of boys.) His father worked abroad and his mother also sold food in the city.

Mark went home in 2013 and remained there with his family. He re-enrolled at school and completed his final year. He planned to attend college. He was solvent free. He stated he was attending church again. However, in 2016 Facebook revealed that Mark was living with a girlfriend, they appear to have two children!

Joel (12)

Joel was the leader of the younger group and had a lot of influence over the others. He was also using solvents daily. He had a good brain and used it to maintain control and to manipulate people. He had a family (dad, step-mother, and three half-siblings) living about thirty minutes away from the bridge area. He was upset about the break- up of his parent's marriage, which is the original reason he ran away to the street.

Joel left rehab in 2014 having made a profession of faith. He returned to the Centre for Youth in Olongapo and was studying. In 2016, he sent me this message

"I am doing Ok, I am currently studying in ALS (Alternative Learning System) and residing at the Youth Centre. My family is doing well. I asked for forgiveness to Jesus Christ and to you too. How are you Ma'am Natalie? I am deeply sorry for all the bad things I did to you. I know it is hard to restore the trust. Thank you for all the love that you have given us. Someday you will see me doing good in life and I will never forget the love you have shown me."

Adam (15)

Adam became one of our regular boys, although we didn't see him much at first. He had some kind of learning difficulty and always seemed to be alone. He was upset that his family had sent him to live with his uncle and "just thrown him away like a piece of rubbish." His uncle gave him money daily for food and sometimes he disappeared for a few days, probably returning to his uncle's house. We couldn't locate the uncle. We were unsure of his age and he didn't know it either. He was also abusing solvents.

Adam left rehab in 2014 after over a year spent in residence there. He had requested to stay for another year, having developed a strong bond with one of the Christian social workers, but later changed his mind when she felt that she needed to tell him that she couldn't be with him all of the time. Adam really just wanted his own family. He returned to the Centre for Youth in Olongapo and continued his studies for a while but in 2017 I heard that he had ended up in a local jail.

Simon (12)

Simon was one of our regular boys and was definitely the one with the cheekiest grin. He was well liked in the group and had had a better upbringing than some of the others. His parents were separated and his Dad disabled (suffering from polio), resulting in the family struggling to put food on the table. Simon had been collecting plastic to sell but got involved with the "rugby boys" due to peer pressure and failed to return home. Simon was abusing solvents every day.

In 2013, Simon was diagnosed with an enlarged heart due to solvent abuse. He secured a medical release from rehab and returned to live with his father and sister. Olongapo Christian Help and Hope financed his ongoing medical costs and a new roof for the family house.

In 2017, Simon informed me that he is doing well, he is medication free and living at the Centre for Youth and attending school. Sadly, his mother died recently. Simon has made a profession of faith.

Solomon (11)

Solomon was with us every day to start with, and we helped him with a medical incident. Shortly after that, in August 2012, he left the bridge and went back to school for a while. He was from a poorer area outside the city and he had eight siblings. The family didn't have enough food. He was abusing solvents daily.

In late 2013, Solomon re-appeared on the street and was sent to the rehab in March 2014. He has been released from rehab and returned home.

Reuben (11)

Reuben was different to some of the other boys because he was a lot younger in himself and really just wanted to play games all of the time. He had been on and off the street since he was just seven. His family lived a long way from the area and he suffered from physical violence at home. He had a stubborn streak though, which was hard to combat at times, but he was also very likeable.

Reuben almost settled with our Christian family, but became restless and ran away. He also escaped from the Centre for Youth a number of times and returned to locate his family, only to find they had moved away and he didn't know where they had gone. He was transferred to the rehab in 2014 and I believe released in early 2016 but is currently spending his second period in rehab.

Joshua (10)

Joshua was the youngest boy abusing solvents. He was Muslim, but we only discovered that after working with the boys for some time. He had family locally and sometimes disappeared for a week when his father caught him and took him home, but he was harshly punished and escaped again as soon as he could.

I was informed that Joshua's family had moved to Manila, having been made homeless in Olongapo. In 2015 I saw Joshua and chatted with him at the local market. He was living back with his family, solvent free and studying.

Luke (15)

Luke was one of the saddest cases because he had a genuine reason for being on the street. He was from a Muslim family and his father had died the previous year. He had only been on the street since his father died but hadn't been to school for many years. His family was extremely poor and lived in cramped conditions with many relatives. He was a likeable boy and he often looked after the younger boys, but he was also easily influenced in a negative way and was addicted to the solvents.

Luke moved to Manila with his mother in 2013 to attend an Islamic school. My last contact with him in 2013 was online when he said he was unhappy and wanted to come back to Olongapo. He also told me that he wasn't in school, but I haven't heard anything from him since. I pray that he is doing well now.

Malachi (9)

Malachi wasn't using solvents when I first met him in 2012, and he only appeared a few times at the bridge. He was often misrepresenting his physical condition in order to beg from local people. Malachi began using solvents in 2013 and was taken to the Centre for Youth and then transferred to rehab having run away from the Centre back to the street several times. He was the youngest boy from Olongapo at the rehab.

Isaac (11)

Isaac was one of the toughest of the younger boys and didn't like to show his affection for us. He only appeared at the bridge a few times during our ministry. He had wealthy family connections, but his parents were separated and there were problems at home. He was often in a different part of town abusing solvents alone.

Isaac was taken to the Centre for Youth and later transferred to Rehab with Solomon in March 2014. The initial shock immediately broke his hard exterior. He was released in 2015.

Paul (14)

Paul was probably the boy that changed the most during our time working with the group. Paul was aggressive, obnoxious, and difficult to handle at first. He just used us for what he could get and constantly tested our boundaries. He had been on and off the street since he was seven. His mother left when he was a baby and his father took solvents, developed mental health problems, and later went to prison. Paul was left in the care of an older couple in the neighbourhood, but the male later died. Paul ran away from one Christian orphanage due to bullying. He was addicted to solvents and had spent a year in rehab at the age of eleven. He was diagnosed with TB at the hospital with us in 2012.

Over time, Paul changed his attitude towards us and became very loyal. He decided to leave the street and made a profession of faith. He lived with our Christian family for several months but made a foolish decision to run away and was caught and sent to rehab in Manila. Paul left rehab in 2014 after being diagnosed with Hepatitis B. He lived at my church in Cubao for a period but missed his family and friends in Olongapo. He returned to Olongapo in early 2015. Sadly, in 2017 I was informed that he was incarcerated at the local jail.

Natalie's Story

I became a Christian at a young age primarily due to having been raised in a Christian home and being surrounded by Christianity. As a teenager there were times when I was really serious about my faith but I often became distracted. During a more serious faith phase at the age of seventeen, I was baptised, but just six weeks later fell away from God in dramatic fashion.

I subsequently spent six years immersed in the "party lifestyle", succumbing to many activities and bad habits that sought to replace God, including an abundance of alcohol, cigarettes and gambling. I moved from one non-Christian relationship to another in an attempt to find the happiness that eluded me. I became more and more miserable, attempting to ignore God but knowing deep down that He was there and that I was under His judgement because of my lifestyle choices.

In the year 2000, I began a degree course in Law and Criminology, but dropped out after just six weeks to join the police, thereby fulfilling a childhood dream. In 2002, my younger brother James (who was a Christian) was tragically killed in a car accident at the age of just eighteen. My parents clung to their Christian faith at this time, but I became angry with God for allowing this to happen and resented Christians for judging my lifestyle.

In April 2005, after many other problems and a long struggle, I faced up to the fact that I was miserable and that my life was a total mess. I had recently witnessed my younger sister, Lauren, going through some of the same struggles. I then saw the resulting contentment when she turned back to God. I knew that I was carrying the heavy weight of my many sins around on my shoulders. I sometimes woke up at night in a terrified state, believing I was going to Hell because of the things I had done. I knew that God was waiting for me to repent of my sins and turn back to Him, and that He had been patiently waiting for a long time. I lived in constant fear that time would run out and that I may have tested God one too many times.

Eventually, like the prodigal son in Luke chapter 15, I realised I couldn't continue as I was and I came to my senses. I said sorry to God for my many sins and asked for His help. I believed the promise that "everyone who calls on the name of the Lord will be saved."

I abandoned my sinful vices immediately and began regularly attending my former church, Worthing Tabernacle. Two Bible verses became very important to me as a result of my experiences. The first is found in John 6:67-68: "'You do not want to leave too, do you?' Jesus asked the Twelve. Simon Peter answered him, 'Lord, to whom shall we go? You have the words of eternal life.'" (NIV) These verses remind me that seeking anyone other than Jesus is a total waste of time because He is the only one with the words of eternal life that can offer hope for the future. The second verse is from Mark 8:36: "For what shall it profit a man, if he shall gain the whole world, and lose his own soul?" (KJV) This sums up my life experience as I tried seeking happiness in the world but foolishly risked losing my soul in the process.

God already had His hand on my life, due to my Christian upbringing, former beliefs and the fact that many people were praying for me regularly. All of the glory for the change in my life goes to God as I wasn't capable of turning my own life around having tried and failed many times.

The Wordless Book

Just in case there are any non-believers reading this, I would like to explain how to become a Christian and how you too can be free of your sin and reconciled to God to spend eternity in Heaven with Him one day.

During my few years of missionary service, I was taught a tool to explain the Gospel. It has been effectively used by millions of people around the world. It is called the "Wordless Book" and consists simply of five coloured sheets of paper, or material each representing part of the message of salvation found in the Bible:

YELLOW

This represents Heaven. Do you want everlasting life in Heaven? The Bible tells us that the streets in Heaven are paved with gold. It also tells us that God is light and that in Him there is no darkness and that Jesus (God's only Son) is the light of the world. Heaven is God's dwelling place and the Bible also tells us that no man has ever imagined the wonderful things that God has prepared in heaven for those that love Him. Heaven is forever.

BLACK

This represents sin. What is wrong with the world? More importantly, what is wrong with me? Being honest, we need to face the bad news in order to see the value of the good news. The Bible says that all people have sinned and fall short of the glory of God and that the wages of sin is death. God is holy and cannot have anything to do with sin. God is righteous and just and, therefore, cannot just overlook our sin and forgive us because this would make Him unjust. Our sin separates us from God's love permanently. All sinners are destined to spend an eternity in Hell under the wrath of God. Hell is a truly terrible place where people will long to die because of their torment but will be unable to do so. Hell is forever. This is the bad news.

RED

This represents the blood of Jesus. Why did Jesus need to die? God loved us so much that He provided a way of for us to be reconciled to Him and to escape the torments of Hell. He sent Jesus, His only son, to live a perfect life here on Earth. It was necessary for a penalty to be paid for our sin. Jesus' purpose in coming was to die for the sins of the world so that anyone who who believes in Him can get to Heaven. He died instead of us so that we could be free from the guilty sentence hanging over us because of our sin. He died on that cross and then rose from the grave just three days later, proving that He had defeated sin and death once and for all. Jesus' death acted as a bridge between guilty sinners and God, allowing all who trust in Him to be forgiven of their sins and to live in Heaven forever with God.

WHITE

This represents being washed clean from sin. How can be we sure of God's acceptance? Think of your life as a white sheet. Every time you sin, even in a small way, a black stain is left on the sheet. When a person becomes a Christian and turns away from their sin, God promises them a new start. He says that he will remember their sins no more. When God looks at the life of a Christian, he sees only Jesus and His righteousness instead of the sin.

GREEN

This represents growth. How should this change my life? All true Christians will grow spiritually over time. In order to grow, Christians should regularly read the word of God (the Bible), pray, attend a church, spend time with other Christians, and tell other people about Jesus and His sacrifice for them. These things do not save people. There are no "divine scales" weighing good and bad deeds as a determining factor for entry to Heaven or Hell. No human can ever do enough good things to get to Heaven, as the standard required is perfection; this is why Jesus had to die. The things described here are the grateful response of a Christian who has been rescued from a life of sin and death and has been reconciled to God for a life of hope and an eternal future in heaven.

Asian Adventures, Cultural Catastrophes, Help and Hope
On-board the World's Largest Floating Book-Fair!

The LOGOS Life

LOGOS HOPE

Natalie Vellacott

A MISSIONARY IN MANILA

NATALIE VELLACOTT

Printed in Great Britain
by Amazon

40673448R00116